Cost-of-Living Crisis

Editor: Danielle Lobban

Volume 448

First published by Independence Educational Publishers

The Studio, High Green

Great Shelford

Cambridge CB22 5EG

England

© Independence 2024

Copyright

This book is sold subject to the condition that it shall not, by way of trade or otherwise, be lent, resold, hired out or otherwise circulated in any form of binding or cover other than that in which it is published without the publisher's prior consent.

Photocopy licence

The material in this book is protected by copyright. However, the purchaser is free to make multiple copies of particular articles for instructional purposes for immediate use within the purchasing institution. Making copies of the entire book is not permitted.

ISBN-13: 978 1 86168 908 5

Printed in Great Britain

Pureprint Group

Acknowledgements

The publisher is grateful for permission to reproduce the material in this book. While every care has been taken to trace and acknowledge copyright, the publisher tenders its apology for any accidental infringement or where copyright has proved untraceable. The publisher would be pleased to come to a suitable arrangement in any such case with the rightful owner.

The material reproduced in **issues** books is provided as an educational resource only. The views, opinions and information contained within reprinted material in **issues** books do not necessarily represent those of Independence Educational Publishers and its employees.

Although every effort has been made to ensure that website addresses are correct at time of going to press, Independence Educational Publishers cannot be held responsible for the content of any website mentioned in this book.

Images

Cover image courtesy of iStock. All other images courtesy of Freepik, Pixabay, Pexels, and Unsplash.

Additional acknowledgements

With thanks to the Independence team: Janey Hills, Klaudia Sommer and Jackie Staines.

Danielle Lobban

Cambridge, October 2024

Contents

Chapter 1: What is Poverty?

What is poverty?	1
What causes poverty?	2
Poverty in the UK: statistics	4
UK Poverty 2024	6

Chapter 2: Cost-of-Living

What is the cost-of-living crisis?	11
300,000 more UK children fell into absolute poverty at height of cost-of-living crisis	14
The cost-of-living conundrum	16
What the cost-of-living crisis looks like around the world	18
'People buy spectacularly less': inflation-hit Europe weighs costs ahead of elections	20
How the cost-of-living crisis affects young people around the world	24
Is the cost-of-living crisis over and will prices in the UK ever come down?	26

Chapter 3: Poverty in the UK

Types of poverty	29
The problem is poverty, however we label it	30
What is food poverty?	32
Food banks in the UK	33
'They don't have enough' – schools in England are running food banks for families	34
More school children to arrive in school with 'dirty clothes and unbrushed teeth' amid increase in hygiene poverty	35
Wet wipe showers and washing up liquid for shampoo: How it feels to live in hygiene poverty	36
Cost of living: UK period poverty has risen from 12% to 21% in a year	38
How is the cost-of-living crisis affecting period poverty in the UK?	39
Where can I find help?	41
Further Reading/Useful Websites	42
Glossary	43
Index	44

Introduction

Cost-of-Living Crisis is volume 448 in the **issues** series. The aim of the series is to offer current, diverse information about important issues in our world, from a UK perspective.

About *Cost-of-Living Crisis*

One in five people in the UK live below the poverty line. This book explores the issue of poverty in the UK and around the world, it examines the causes and effects of poverty on families and communities, as well as ongoing efforts to eliminate it.

Our sources

Titles in the **issues** series are designed to function as educational resource books, providing a balanced overview of a specific subject.

The information in our books is comprised of facts, articles and opinions from many different sources, including:

- Newspaper reports and opinion pieces
- Website factsheets
- Magazine and journal articles
- Statistics and surveys
- Government reports
- Literature from special interest groups.

A note on critical evaluation

Because the information reprinted here is from a number of different sources, readers should bear in mind the origin of the text and whether the source is likely to have a particular bias when presenting information (or when conducting their research). It is hoped that, as you read about the many aspects of the issues explored in this book, you will critically evaluate the information presented.

It is important that you decide whether you are being presented with facts or opinions. Does the writer give a biased or unbiased report? If an opinion is being expressed, do you agree with the writer? Is there potential bias to the 'facts' or statistics behind an article?

Activities

Throughout this book, you will find a selection of assignments and activities designed to help you engage with the articles you have been reading and to explore your own opinions. Some tasks will take longer than others and there is a mixture of design, writing and research-based activities that you can complete alone or in a group.

Further research

At the end of each article we have listed its source and a website that you can visit if you would like to conduct your own research. Please remember to critically evaluate any sources that you consult and consider whether the information you are viewing is accurate and unbiased.

Issues Online

The **issues** series of books is complemented by our online resource, issuesonline.co.uk

On the Issues Online website you will find a wealth of information, covering over 75 topics, to support the PSHE and RSE curriculum.

Why Issues Online?

Researching a topic? Issues Online is the best place to start for...

Librarians

Issues Online is an essential tool for librarians: feel confident you are signposting safe, reliable, user-friendly online resources to students and teaching staff alike. We provide multi-user concurrent access, so no waiting around for another student to finish with a resource. Issues Online also provides FREE downloadable posters for your shelf/wall/table displays.

Teachers

Issues Online is an ideal resource for lesson planning, inspiring lively debate in class, and setting lessons and homework tasks.

Our accessible, engaging content helps deepen students' knowledge, promotes critical thinking, and develops independent learning skills.

Issues Online saves precious preparation time. We wade through the wealth of material on the internet to filter the best quality, most relevant and up-to-date information you need to start exploring a topic.

Our carefully selected, balanced content presents an overview and insight into each topic from a variety of sources and viewpoints.

Students

Issues Online is designed to support your studies in a broad range of topics, particularly social issues relevant to young people today.

There are thousands of articles, statistics and infographs instantly available to help you with homework, research, and assignments.

With 24/7 access using the powerful Algolia search system, you can find relevant information quickly, easily and safely anytime from your laptop, tablet or smartphone, in class or at home.

Visit issuesonline.co.uk to find out more!

Chapter 1

What is Poverty?

What is poverty?

When we hear the word 'poverty,' images of hunger, homelessness, and desperation often come to mind. But what does it really mean to live in poverty in the UK today? Understanding poverty is important because it affects millions of people, including teenagers. So, let's dive into what poverty is, how it's measured, and what life is like for those struggling to make ends meet.

Defining poverty

Poverty is about not having enough money to meet basic needs such as food, clothing, and shelter. However, it's not just about survival; poverty also involves a lack of resources to participate fully in society. It means not being able to heat your home, afford a balanced diet, or have the same opportunities as your peers. Essentially, poverty can stop you from reaching your full potential.

In the UK, poverty can be defined in several ways. The most common are absolute poverty and relative poverty. Absolute poverty is when a person's resources are below a fixed level – it is an unchanging line, usually set at a certain level of income. This is the line beneath which a person is unable to afford basic human needs.

Relative poverty, on the other hand, is a measure of inequality. It refers to how a person's income or resources compare with the average in society. In the UK, you're considered to be in relative poverty if your household income is less than 60% of the median (middle) UK income after housing costs are taken into account.

Causes of poverty

Several factors can cause or contribute to poverty in the UK. These can include:

- Unemployment or underemployment: Without steady work or enough hours, it's challenging to make enough money to cover necessities.
- Low wages: For those earning minimum wage or just above, it can be tough to make ends meet, especially in regions where the cost-of-living is high.
- Lack of education or skills: Without certain qualifications or training, higher-paying jobs may be out of reach.
- Health issues: Long-term health problems can prevent people from working or lead to high medical expenses.
- Debt: High levels of debt can eat into the money available for other needs.
- Housing costs: Rising rents and the scarcity of affordable housing can take a huge bite out of budgets.
- Family structure: Single-parent families, for instance, might struggle with the combination of childcare responsibilities and work.

The impact of poverty

Living in poverty means dealing with a variety of challenges. Food insecurity is one of them, where families might not know where their next meal is coming from. Poor housing conditions and overcrowding can also be an issue, leading to health problems and a lack of space for children to study or play. In many cases, poverty can affect education, as children from low-income families may not have the resources for necessary school materials or extracurricular activities.

The stress of living in poverty can also have a significant impact on mental health. It can create a sense of shame, as societal stigma often accompanies poverty, making people feel like they are to blame for their situation. This can be particularly tough on teenagers, who may feel different from their peers due to their family's financial situation.

What causes poverty?

Poverty is a complex issue with various underlying causes. It is often characterised by a lack of access to essential resources and an inability to meet basic needs. Poverty can be classified into two main categories: absolute poverty, which refers to the inability to afford the bare minimum for survival, and relative poverty, which is the condition of having fewer resources and opportunities compared to others in society. In this article, we will explore several key causes of poverty, examining how they contribute to its perpetuation and discussing their impact on individuals and communities.

What are some of the causes of poverty in the UK?

Low levels of skills or education:

One significant cause of poverty is the low levels of skills or education among individuals. A lack of access to quality education and limited opportunities for skill development can severely limit job prospects and income potential. Without the necessary skills to compete in the job market, individuals may find themselves trapped in low-wage or unstable employment, perpetuating the cycle of poverty. Additionally, limited educational opportunities hinder personal and professional growth, making it challenging to escape the grasp of poverty.

Unemployment:

Unemployment is one of the main causes of poverty. When individuals are unable to secure regular employment, they face difficulties in meeting their basic needs and providing for their families. Long-term unemployment can also have detrimental effects on an individual's sense of self-worth and mental wellbeing, exacerbating the impact of poverty. High levels of unemployment are often influenced by broader economic factors, such as recessions or lack of job opportunities in specific industries.

Low-paid jobs:

Low-paid jobs reinforce poverty by failing to provide individuals with a sufficient income to meet their needs. Many individuals, particularly those without higher levels of education or specialised skills, may find themselves stuck in jobs that offer minimum wage or below. This inability to earn a livable wage further exacerbates poverty, perpetuating a vicious cycle. Limited income also restricts access to essential services, healthcare, and educational opportunities, making it increasingly challenging to escape poverty.

Jobs lacking security or prospects:

Jobs lacking security or future prospects contribute significantly to poverty. Many individuals work in precarious

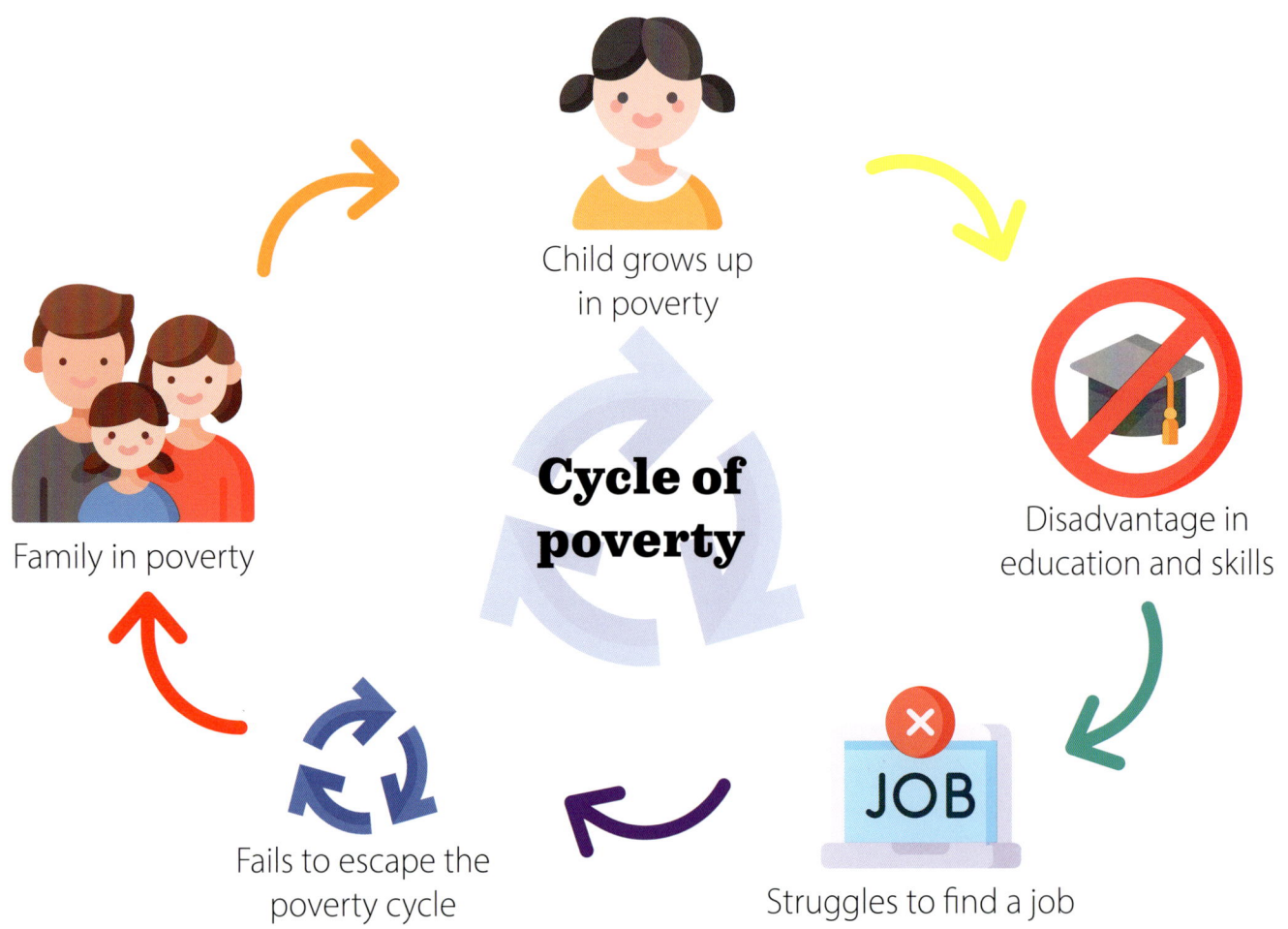

employment situations, such as temporary or contract positions, which often lack stability and consistent income. Without secure employment, individuals face difficulties in planning for the future, saving money, or accessing benefits like health insurance or retirement plans. The uncertainty of such jobs makes it challenging to break the cycle of poverty and improve one's circumstances.

The benefit system:

The design and effectiveness of the benefit system also play a crucial role in perpetuating or alleviating poverty. Inadequate welfare support can leave vulnerable populations without the means to meet their basic needs. A lack of access to social safety nets, combined with stringent eligibility criteria, can contribute to significant disparities in wealth distribution. A well-designed benefit system that provides adequate assistance, promotes self-sufficiency, and offers support in times of crisis can help address poverty and break its cycle.

High cost-of-living:

The high cost-of-living, including the rising prices of housing, healthcare, and other essential services, is a major contributor to poverty. When the cost of these basic necessities outpaces income growth, individuals and families are forced to make difficult choices, often sacrificing crucial needs. As the cost-of-living rises, those facing poverty are disproportionately affected, as they have limited financial resources to meet their basic needs, leading to an increased risk of homelessness, food insecurity, and health problems.

Financial education:

Not knowing how to manage money can make it hard to escape poverty. Many people don't learn basic financial skills at home or in school, like how to budget, save, or avoid debt. Without these skills, teens and adults might end up with credit card debt, loans they can't repay, or poor credit scores, all of which can make life tougher. Learning about money management early on helps people make better financial decisions, like saving for big expenses or avoiding unnecessary debt. If schools included financial education, teens could better understand things like saving, credit, and planning for the future. This knowledge can give people the confidence and ability to make choices that lead to financial stability and independence.

Discrimination:

Discrimination, whether based on race, gender, or other factors, can also perpetuate poverty. Marginalised groups may face systemic barriers and unequal opportunities, limiting their chances of obtaining stable employment or accessing better education and healthcare. Discrimination creates social and economic disadvantages that contribute to poverty rates within affected communities. Addressing these injustices is crucial to breaking the cycle of poverty and promoting equitable opportunities for all.

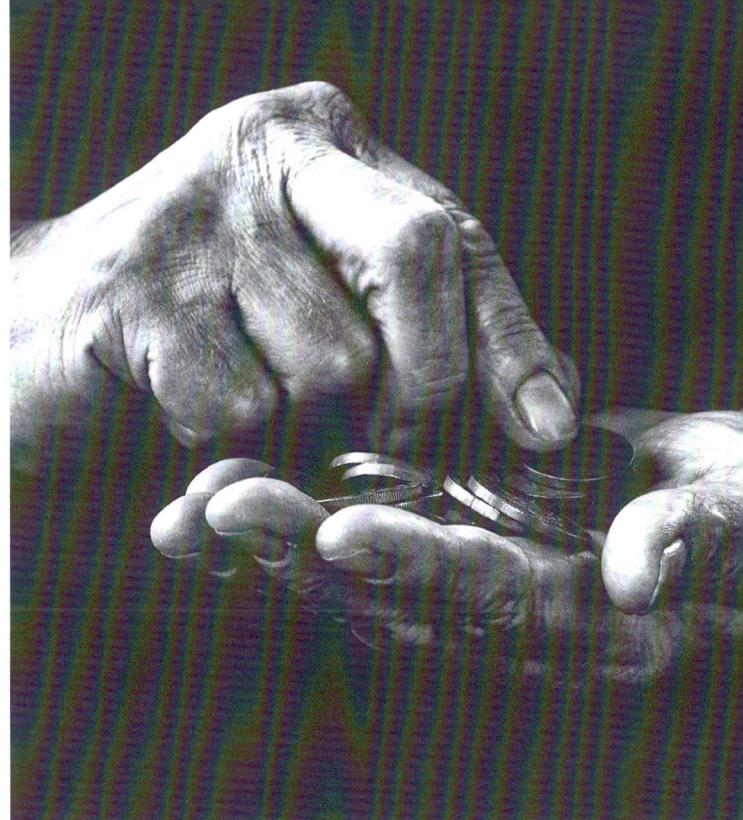

Relationships:

Relationship dynamics and family circumstances can also be a factor in the perpetuation of poverty. Poverty can strain relationships, leading to increased stress and conflict within families. Additionally, individuals born into impoverished households may face limited access to resources and opportunities, making it more challenging to rise above their circumstances. The intergenerational transmission of poverty can result from limited social mobility and a lack of support systems.

Abuse or trauma:

The impact of abuse or trauma should not be underestimated as a contributing factor to poverty. Individuals who have experienced trauma may struggle with mental health issues, addiction, or physical health problems, making it difficult to maintain stable employment or access support systems. These challenges can further exacerbate poverty, as individuals may face difficulties in finding employment or obtaining education, leaving them vulnerable to long-term economic hardship.

Consequences of poverty on people's lives

Poverty affects many parts of life, not just money. People who are poor often struggle with high stress, poor health, limited education, and fewer job opportunities. They may also face food insecurity and even homelessness. Poverty can continue for generations, making it harder for families to break free and deepening social inequality. To tackle poverty, it's important to address causes like low education levels, unemployment, low-paying jobs, high living costs, and discrimination. By creating fair access to education, jobs, and support systems, we can help reduce poverty and build a fairer society.

Poverty in the UK: statistics

This briefing explains UK poverty statistics, including historical trends and forecasts, and poverty by employment, tenure, ethnicity, disability and region.

By Brigid Francis-Devine

How is poverty measured?

The focus in this briefing is on poverty defined in terms of disposable household income (income after adding on benefits and deducting direct taxes). However, poverty may be defined in different ways and there is no single, universally accepted definition.

Two commonly used measures of poverty based on disposable income are:

- Relative low income: This refers to people living in households with income below 60% of the median in that year.

- Absolute low income: This refers to people living in households with income below 60% of median income in a base year, usually 2010/11. This measurement is adjusted for inflation.

Median income is the point at which half of households have lower income and half have higher income.

Income can be measured before or after housing costs are deducted.

How will the rising cost-of-living affect poverty?

High inflation meant real (inflation-adjusted) median household incomes fell in 2022/23. In March 2024 the Office for Budget Responsibility forecasted that real household disposable incomes per head will increase by 0.1% in 2024 and then by 1.7% in 2025. Based on these forecasts, real post-tax income per person will not return to its pre-pandemic level (Q4 2019) until Q4 2025. The OBR is an independent fiscal watchdog that analyses public finances and fiscal policy.

Absolute low income increased by 500,000 people before housing costs and 600,000 people after housing costs in the year to 2022/23. Absolute low income is likely to continue to rise in the short run: the Resolution Foundation forecasted in September 2023 that absolute poverty will increase by 300,000, from 11.7 million in 2023/24 to 12.0 million in 2024/25. This will bring the rate to 18.0% in 2024/25, the same rate as 2019/20.

This is because real incomes are set to fall, and income is adjusted for inflation when measuring absolute low income.

Since relative low income compares low income households to median income, the fact that income is set to fall for everyone means that relative low income is likely to fall between 2022/23 and 2023/24.

However, the Resolution Foundation expects relative child poverty to return to its upward trend at the end of the cost-of-living crisis and reach its highest levels since 1998/99 in 2027/28.

How many people are in poverty?

Department for Work and Pensions (DWP) data shows that around one in six people in the UK were in relative low income (relative poverty) before housing costs in 2022/23. This rises to just over one in five people once housing costs are accounted for.

Relative low income in the UK in 2022/23

11.4 million people (17%) were in relative poverty before housing costs and 14.3 million after housing costs (21%). This includes 3.2 million children (22%) before housing costs and 4.3 million after housing costs (30%).

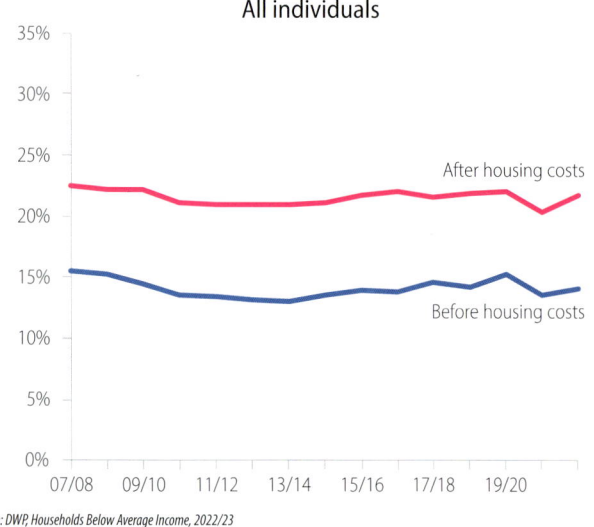

The % of people in relative low income in 2022/23 was at a similar level to before the pandemic

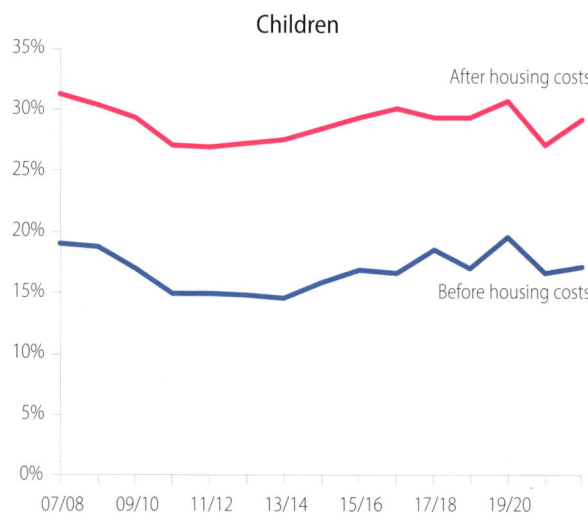

Relative child poverty was also around the same as pre-pandemic levels

Source: DWP, Households Below Average Income, 2022/23

Absolute low income in the UK in 2022/23

9.5 million people (14%) were in absolute low income before housing costs and 12.0 million after housing costs (18%). This includes 2.6 million children (18%) before housing costs and 3.6 million after housing costs (25%).

The % of people in absolute low income has been fairly steady over the past few years.

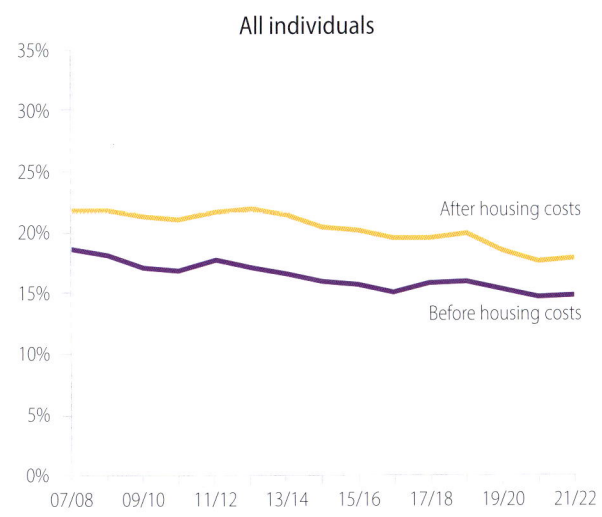

Absolute low income is forecasted to rise due to high inflation

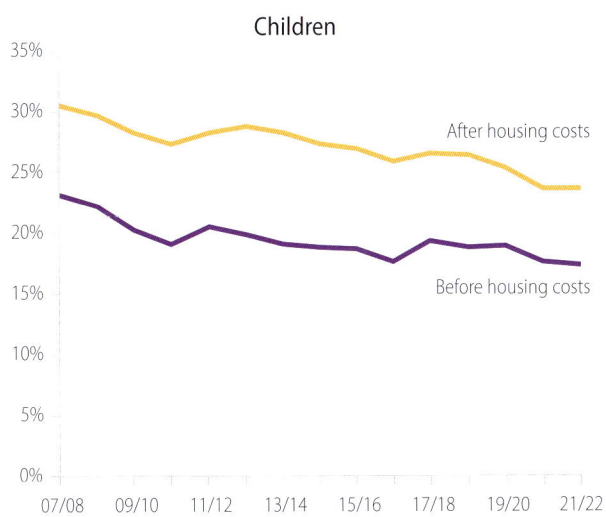

Source: DWP, Households Below Average Income, 2022/23

14% of people in the UK were in absolute low income before housing costs in 2022/23, and 18% were in absolute low income (absolute poverty) after housing costs.

Over the longer-term, poverty rates have reduced since the late 1990s for children, pensioners, and working-age parents. However, for working-age adults without dependent children the likelihood of being in relative low income has increased.

Food insecurity and material deprivation rose sharply in 2022/23

The number of people in food insecure households rose by around 2.5 million between 2021/22 and 2022/23, from 4.7 million to 7.2 million. This means 11% of people lived in food insecure households in 2022/23, including 17% of children.

1.9 million children were in relative low income (below 70% of median income) and material deprivation in 2022/23, 13% of children in the UK. This is up from 1.6 million in 2021/22.

Who is in poverty?

Some groups are more likely than others to be in poverty.

In 2022/23, relative poverty rates were highest for people in households where the head of the household is from the Pakistani or Bangladeshi ethnic groups and lowest for those from White ethnic groups.

Around 37% of working-age adults in workless families were in relative poverty before housing costs in 2022/23, compared to 10% in families where at least one adult was in work.

44% of social renters and 35% of private renters were in relative low income after housing costs in 2022/23, compared to 14% of people who owned their home outright and 10% of those who have a mortgage.

The proportion of people in relative low income before housing costs (BHC) was 24% for families where someone is disabled, compared to 15% for people living in families where no one is disabled.

Other ways of thinking about poverty

There is debate about whether income is the best way to measure poverty. The Social Metrics Commission (SMC), which looks at poverty measurements, proposed basing the measure on the extent that someone's resources meet their needs. This accounts for differences among households such as costs of childcare and disability, savings, and access to assets. The DWP are developing a new measure called Below Average Resources (BAR), using the framework suggested by the SMC.

A research project funded by the Joseph Rowntree Foundation, a poverty charity, estimates a Minimum Income Standard: the level of income needed to meet a minimum acceptable standard of living each year.

Measures like material deprivation and destitution provide an insight on how many people are unable to afford essentials.

8 April 2024

The above information is reprinted with kind permission from UK Parliament.
© UK Parliament 2024
This information is licensed under the Open Parliament Licence v3.0
To view this licence, visit https://www.parliament.uk/site-information/copyright-parliament/open-parliament-licence/

www.parliament.uk

UK Poverty 2024

The UK is entering this election year with unacceptably high levels of poverty, appallingly high for some groups. We need a coherent plan with creative policies to end poverty in the UK.

This report looks at the current situation across different groups and regions, and the future prospects for poverty in the UK.

UK Poverty uses a range of data sources and insights to build up a comprehensive picture of the current state of poverty across the UK. As poverty can lead to negative impacts at all stages of life, this report tells us who is worst affected, how levels have changed over time and what the future prospects might be.

Since last year's report, we have seen even more evidence of the desperate measures that households are having to take to get by, and of the high tides of insecurity that have washed over more and more people.

Below is a summary of the key findings of the UK Poverty 2024 report.

Poverty has increased, close to pre-pandemic levels

More than 1 in 5 people in the UK (22%) were in poverty in 2021/22 – 14.4 million people. This included:

- 8.1 million (or around 2 in 10) working-age adults
- 4.2 million (or nearly 3 in 10) children
- 2.1 million (or around 1 in 6) pensioners.

Poverty rates have returned to around their pre-pandemic levels, as middle-income household incomes rose at the same time as a range of temporary coronavirus-related support was withdrawn.

It has been almost 20 years and 6 prime ministers since the last prolonged period of falling poverty

The overall level of poverty has barely moved since Conservative-led governments took power in 2010. Poverty last fell consistently during the first half of the last Labour administration (between 1999/2000 and 2004/05), but then rose in the second half of their time in power. In part, this reflects the hits to living standards that have affected everyone, from the economic slowdown even before the global financial crisis to the current cost-of-living crisis.

Before 1979, levels of poverty had been broadly flat at around 14%. In the 1980s, under the Conservative Government of Margaret Thatcher, there was then an unprecedented rise in poverty even at a time of high income growth, due to very unequal income growth over this period. This has not been reversed, meaning current levels of poverty are around 50% higher than they were in the 1970s.

Poverty is deepening

In 2021/22, 6 million people – or 4 in 10 people in poverty – were in 'very deep' poverty, with an income far below the standard poverty line. More than twice as many (over 12 million people) had experienced very deep poverty in at least one year between 2017–18 and 2020–21.

Children have consistently had the highest poverty rates, while pensioners along with working-age adults without children now have the lowest

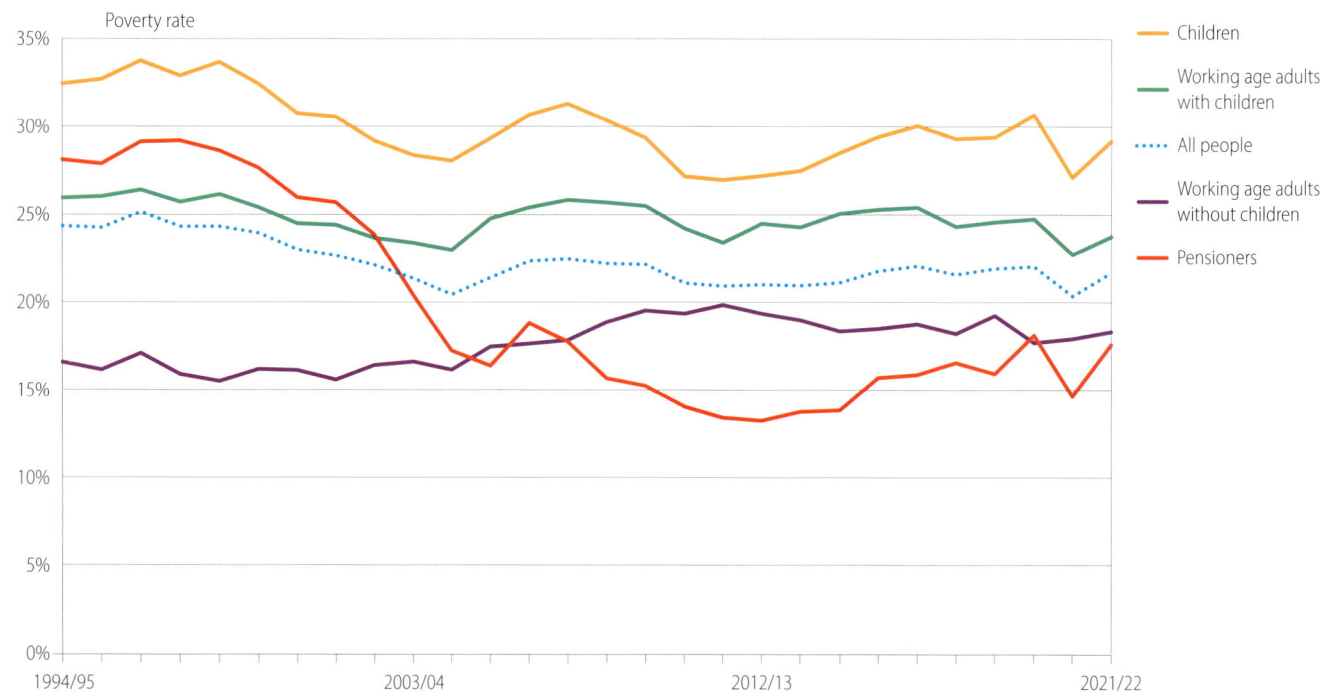

Source: Households Below Average Income, 2021/22, Department for Work and Pensions (DWP)

Poverty rates grew rapidly under Margaret Thatcher's administration and remained high, with only small decreases in subsequent administrations

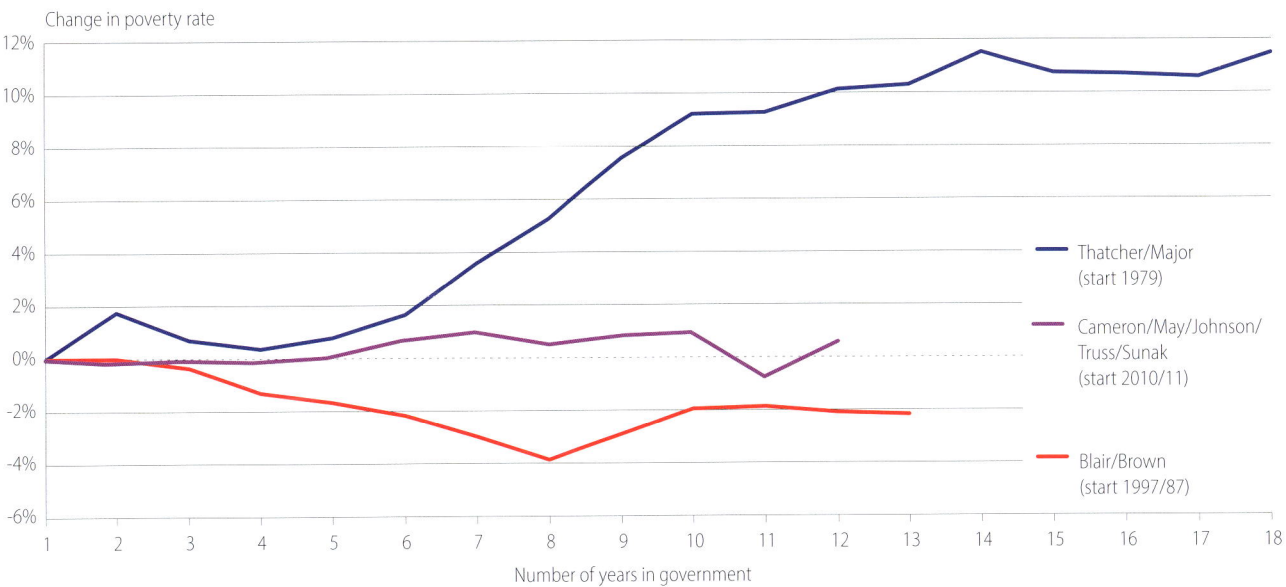

Source: Institute for Fiscal Studies' (2023) analysis of Family Expenditure Survey and Households Below Average Income data

Between 2019/20 and 2021/22, the average person in poverty had an income 29% below the poverty line, with the gap up from 23% between 1994/95 and 1996/97. The poorest families – those living in very deep poverty – had an average income that was 59% below the poverty line, with this gap increasing by around two-thirds over the past 25 years.

This is equivalent to a couple with two children under 14 years old needing, on average:

- an additional £6,200 per year to reach the poverty line if they are living in poverty
- an additional £12,800 per year to reach the poverty line if they are living in very deep poverty.

We saw from our latest Destitution in the UK report that around 3.8 million people experienced destitution (where they could not afford to meet their most basic physical needs to stay warm, dry, clean and fed) in 2022. This included around one million children. These figures have more than doubled since 2017. There is further evidence of deepening poverty in the increasing number of people using food banks, with more emergency food parcels being delivered by the Trussell Trust network than ever before.

Certain groups have wholly unacceptably high rates of poverty

Some groups of people face particularly high levels of poverty. This includes:

- Larger families – 43% of children in families with three or more children were in poverty in 2021/22. A number of benefit policies, including the two-child limit and the benefit cap, have a disproportionate impact on larger families.

- Families whose childcare responsibilities limit their ability to work – 44% of children in lone-parent families were in poverty in 2021/22, as were 32% of children in families where the youngest child was aged under 5.

Since 1994/95, the percentage of people in poverty who are in very deep poverty has increased, and now makes up the largest group of people in poverty

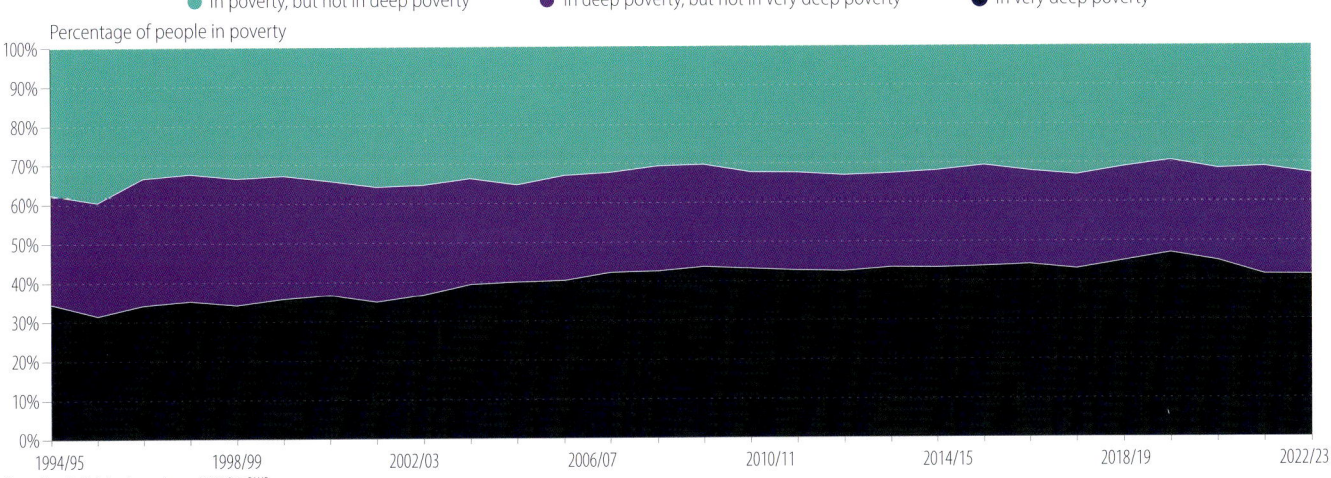

Source: Households Below Average Income, 2021/22, DWP

Note: The group in very deep poverty includes people whose equivalised household income after housing costs (AHC) is less than 40% of median AHC income. The group in deep poverty, but not very deep poverty, have an equivalised AHC household income less than 50% but more than 40% of median AHC income. The group in poverty, but not deep poverty, have an equivalised AHC household income less than 60% but more than 50% of median AHC income

The poverty gap and the deep poverty gap have grown at similar rates since 1994/95–1996/97, but the very deep poverty gap has been consistently larger

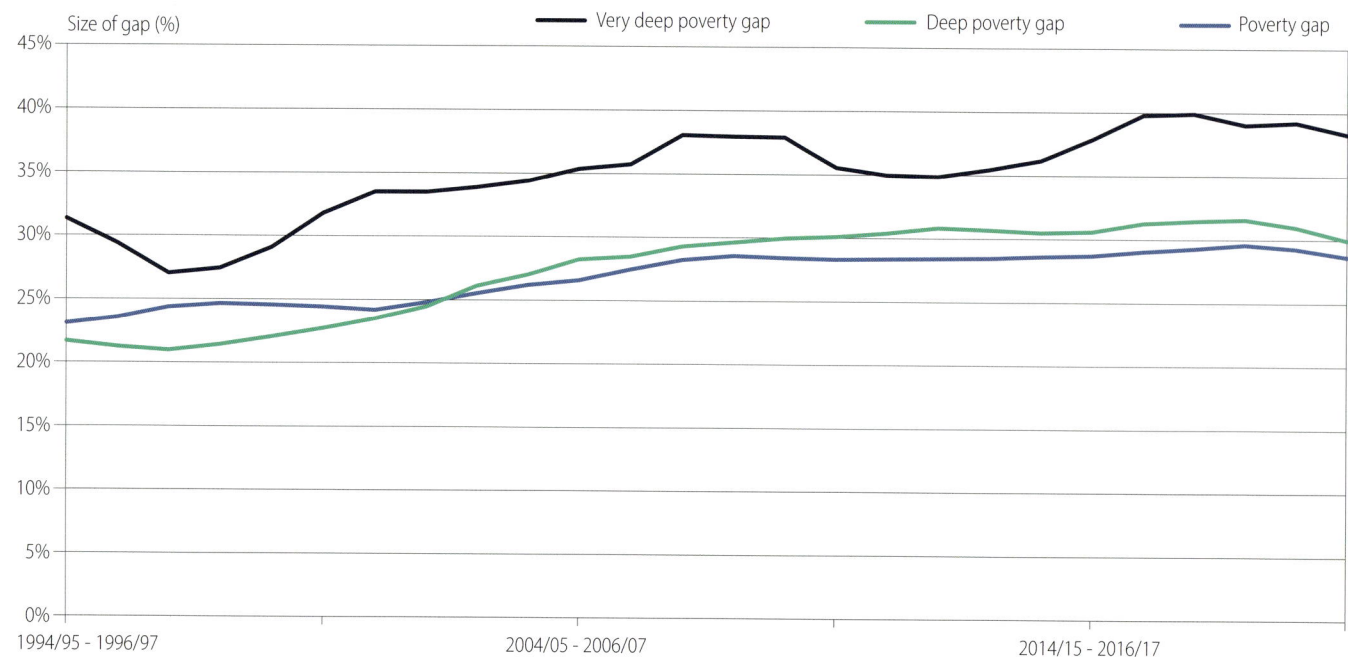

Source: Households Below Average Income, 2021/22, DWP
Note: The poverty gap is the difference between the median equivalised income of people in poverty and the relevant poverty line, as a percentage of the poverty line in each year. The deep poverty gap and very deep poverty gap are calculated using figures for 50% and 40% of the median household income respectively.

- Many minority ethnic groups – around half of people in Pakistani (51%) and Bangladeshi households (53%) and around 4 in 10 people in households headed by someone from an Asian background other than Indian, Pakistani, Bangladeshi or Chinese (39%) or households from Black African backgrounds (42%) were in poverty between 2019/20 and 2021/22. These households also have higher rates of child poverty, very deep poverty and persistent poverty.

- Disabled people – in 2021/22, 31% of disabled people were in poverty. This was even higher (38%) for people with a long-term, limiting mental health condition. Higher poverty rates for disabled people are partly due to the additional costs associated with disability and ill health and partly due to the barriers to work they face.

- Informal carers – 28% of people with caring responsibilities were in poverty in 2021/22. Informal carers face a financial penalty, because of their limited ability to work, with unpaid social-care givers experiencing an average pay penalty of nearly £5,000 a year.

- Families not in work – more than half of working-age adults (56%) in workless households were in poverty in 2021/22, compared with 15% in working households. However, because a high share of the population is in work, around two-thirds of working-age adults in poverty actually lived in a household where someone was in work.

- Part-time workers and the self-employed – amongst people in work, the poverty rate for part-time workers was double that for full-time workers (20% compared with 10%), and self-employed workers were more than twice as likely to be in poverty as employees (23% compared with 10%).

- People living in rented accommodation – in 2021/22, more than 4 in 10 social renters (43%) and around a third of private renters (35%) were in poverty after housing costs. Around a third of these social renters and half of these private renters were only in poverty after their housing costs were factored in, so appear to be pushed into poverty by the amount they have to spend on housing.

- Families claiming income-related benefits – their high poverty rates may be expected given the 'low income' eligibility criteria for claiming these benefits, but it demonstrates that benefit levels are frequently not sufficient to enable recipients to escape poverty. Indeed, the basic rate of Universal Credit is even below destitution thresholds.

Poverty across the UK

Poverty rates vary significantly between UK nations and regions

Between 2019/20 and 2021/22, the average poverty rates in England (22%), Wales (22%) and Scotland (21%) had converged to around the same level, although poverty rates were much lower in Northern Ireland (16%).

Between 2019/20 and 2021/22, the West Midlands had the highest rate of poverty at 27%, followed by the North East and London (both 25%), Yorkshire and The Humber, the East Midlands and the North West (all 23%).

These variations are driven by differences in labour markets, housing markets and rates of benefit receipt, alongside wider demographic factors of the population in each nation or region. The greater reliance on renting and the higher costs of housing are a substantial driver in larger cities in particular (including London), while lower rates of employment, fewer employment opportunities and a greater concentration

of employment in lower-paid roles, are bigger drivers in many post-industrial and coastal areas (including the West Midlands and the North East of England).

Child poverty rates in Scotland (24%) remain much lower than those in England (31%) and Wales (28%) and are similar (if slightly higher) than in Northern Ireland (22%). This is likely to be due, at least in part, to the Scottish Child Payment. This highlights the effect benefits can have in reducing poverty.

Cost-of-living crisis continues to bite

In October 2023, around:

- 2.8 million of the poorest fifth of households (47%) were in arrears with their household bills or behind on scheduled lending repayments
- 4.2 million households (72%) were going without essentials
- 3.4 million households (58%) reported not having enough money for food.

This is why it is so important that the Government has uprated benefits in an appropriate way and has re-established the link between housing support and rents. However, it is very worrying that many of the Government's support schemes are ending, especially when the basic rates of benefits are below destitution levels and millions are going without essentials.

The future remains deeply worrying

Inflation is still running at twice its target level, benefits are taking time to catch up with rising prices, employment is starting to fall, earnings are still below their 2008 levels, and housing costs are increasing rapidly. Given the Office for Budget Responsibility forecasts that average household disposable incomes will continue to fall until 2024/25, these effects will have a profound impact on many people's living standards for years to come.

What can be done?

People recognise the scale of the problem facing the country and the need to take action. The British Social Attitudes survey found that the proportion of people who think there is quite a lot of real poverty in Britain has increased by nearly 20 percentage points since 2006, while the majority of the British public, in surveys since 2017, has agreed that the Government should increase tax and spending on health, education and social benefits. Meanwhile, the cost-of-living crisis is putting pressure on families across the country and in November 2023, our polling found that 73% of the British public were very or fairly worried about the cost of essentials.

We have now experienced nearly three tough years of accelerating inflation and four desperate years since the start of the Covid-19 pandemic. There was little progress on headline poverty and increasing levels of deep poverty and destitution even before then.

In our UK Poverty 2020 report, published immediately before the pandemic, we said:

'For a decent standard of living, we all need security and stability in our lives – secure housing, a reliable income, and support when things get difficult. For too many of us, there is no such security. Millions of people in the UK are struggling to get by, leading insecure and precarious lives, held back from improving their living standards. It's time to take action on poverty and put this right.'

This remains our clarion call and the key test we will be using to evaluate political parties' plans to tackle hardship and expand the foundations of economic security to everyone ahead of the next election. This requires action to reset our social and economic fundamentals, starting with:

- help and space for people looking for work to find a secure job that sticks, while making work possible and desirable for those outside the labour market where possible

- raising the basic level of workplace rights and protections, including expanding rights to flexible working, and improving financial protection for people who lose their job or cannot work

- protecting time for caring around work, while building up and strengthening the infrastructure of care services for families to rely on

- ensuring social security provides enough income to afford the essentials, at the same time as forging a 'social safety net' of crisis support, practical help and connection in people's communities

- making future pension provision more secure, by raising minimum contribution rates and establishing good options for people to use their savings to provide a secure standard of living in retirement

- helping people build up modest savings, access affordable credit, gain relief from problem debt and hold assets

- expanding access to secure homes, whether rented or owned, by building more new homes and shifting the distribution of existing homes.

Beyond this, we need a vision for reducing the level, depth and extremes of poverty across the UK. This requires a suite of policies that make up a coherent overall plan to end poverty in the UK that is proportionate to the size of the challenge we face.

The Government must act with compassion, drawing on the lived experience of people who have gone through hardship. It must also implement creative policy innovations that enable everyone to live with dignity, to be able to seize opportunities and, most importantly, to build a sense of hope for a better future.

23 January 2024

Source: ONS Open Geography Portal, ONS, Households Below Average Income, 2019/20 and 2021/22, DWP

The above information is reprinted with kind permission from the Joseph Rowntree Foundation.

© 2024 Joseph Rowntree Foundation

www.jrf.org.uk

Chapter 2: Cost of Living

What is the cost-of-living crisis?

In recent years, you might have heard a lot about the 'cost-of-living crisis' in the UK, especially in news segments, social media, and even discussions among friends and family. This term refers to the increasing difficulty people face as the cost of everyday essentials like food, energy (gas and electricity), and housing continues to rise, while their incomes don't keep up at the same pace. This squeeze on budgets affects everyone, and it's a key topic that's shaping the country's economic conversations today.

Understanding the basics

Before delving deeper, let's break down what we mean by 'cost-of-living'. Simply put, it refers to the amount of money needed to cover basic expenses such as housing, groceries, taxes, healthcare, and transportation in a specific place and time. The crisis occurs when these costs escalate faster than people's wages and other sources of income, making it increasingly difficult to manage day-to-day expenses.

What's driving the cost-of-living crisis?

Several factors contribute to this phenomenon, some local, while others are global:

1. **Inflation:** Inflation is a significant driver. It's the rate at which the general level of prices for goods and services rises, leading to a fall in purchasing power. For example, if inflation is at 5%, a loaf of bread that cost £1 last year would now be £1.05. This seems small, but when applied to every item and service, it significantly affects total spending.

2. **Energy prices:** The UK has experienced surging energy prices, partly because of increased global demand and geopolitical tensions (such as conflicts in oil-rich regions). Since the country relies heavily on natural gas and electricity for heating and power, spikes in energy costs directly affect households.

3. **Fuel prices**: Over the past decade, the cost of fuels like petrol and diesel has steadily increased. This trend can be attributed to oil producers reducing their output combined with a surge in demand, resulting in the depletion of global fuel reserves. Consequently, this scarcity drives up wholesale prices. The escalation in fuel expenses significantly affects both businesses and individuals. Businesses, faced with higher operational costs, often transfer these additional expenses to consumers in the form of increased prices for goods and services. Similarly, individuals feel the pinch as they are compelled to spend more on commuting and various transportation needs.

4. **Housing costs:** Real estate prices and rental costs have soared in many parts of the UK. Demand surpasses supply, especially in major cities like London, making it harder for people to afford suitable housing.

5. **Brexit:** The exit of the UK from the European Union has had various economic impacts, including increased trading barriers and costs, affecting food prices and availability.

6. **Global pandemic:** Events like the Covid-19 pandemic have disrupted supply chains, leading to shortages and higher prices.

Impact on society

The cost-of-living crisis doesn't affect everyone equally; it hits low-income families the hardest because a larger portion of their income goes to necessities compared to affluent families. For many, this means cutting back on essentials like heating or nutritious food, which can lead to broader social issues, including health problems and reduced educational attainment for young people like yourself.

The global picture

The cost-of-living crisis is not just a problem in the UK; it is happening worldwide. Inflation, which is the rise in prices over time, has affected many countries. In places like the United States and Europe, inflation has reached levels not seen for decades. This means that, much like in the UK, people are having to pay more for everyday items like groceries, fuel, and rent.

One major cause of this global inflation is the Covid-19 pandemic. During the pandemic, economies around the world slowed down. Factories closed, fewer goods were produced, and international trade was disrupted. When economies started to recover, there was a huge demand for goods, but not enough supply. This mismatch between supply and demand pushed up prices.

Another factor is the war in Ukraine, which has affected global supplies of energy and food, particularly wheat and oil. Countries that rely on imports from Ukraine and Russia have seen food and energy prices skyrocket, making it harder for people to afford their daily needs.

Winter Fuel Payments

What was the winter fuel payment?

Introduced in 1997 by a Labour Government the winter fuel payment was given to all people* in England and Wales who claimed their state pension. At first, this was everyone over the age of 60, although this rose to 65 in 2010 and 66 from 2018 until 2024. People living abroad, who were in receipt of a UK state pension were also given the fuel allowance, even those who lived in countries with a milder climate, such as Spain or Portugal.

In winter 2023–2024, payments started at £200 and some people, depending on their circumstances, received as much as £600.

What has happened to the fuel allowance?

In July 2024, the Chancellor Rachel Reeves announced the plan to limit the winter fuel allowance to only those who are in reciept of certain benefits, such as pension credit, as she said there was a need to fill a £22 billion 'black hole' in the public finances left by the previous government. However, as some have pointed out the £22 billion deficit in public finances was been inflated due to the £9 billion public sector pay rises above-inflation which Labour granted.

Cutting the fuel allowance will save around £1.4 billion this year.

What will the consequences be?

In 2017, Labour, who were then in opposition, warned the Conservative Government that plans to cut the allowance for up to 10 million pensioners would increase excess deaths by 3,850 that winter.

Since the introduction of the winter fuel payment 20 years earlier, excess deaths among the elderly in winter fell from around 34,000 to 24,000. Labour also warned that cutting the fuel allowance would also put more pressure on to an already struggling NHS.

some people were/are not eligible such as those who:

- *live in Scotland*
- *have been in hospital getting free treatment for more than a year*
- *were in prison for a certain period*
- *were living in a care home for a certain period.*

Measures to combat the crisis

To address these challenges, both the government and various organisations are stepping in:

- **Government interventions:** The UK Government has introduced schemes like the energy price cap to limit how much energy suppliers can charge per unit of gas or electricity. There were also increases in Universal Credit and other benefits aimed at helping the most vulnerable families cope. The Cost-of-living Payments for recipients of certain benefits started late 2022 and finished in spring 2024.
- **Wage adjustments:** Some employers are raising wages to help employees meet their living costs. However, this is not widespread and depends largely on the sector and individual employer.
- **Community support:** Local food banks, charities, and community groups are vital in offering immediate relief to those hardest hit, providing food parcels, clothing, and other essentials.

The cost-of-living crisis is a complex and challenging situation that requires cooperation and innovative solutions from all sectors of society – government, businesses, and citizens alike. By staying informed and involved, you can contribute to the broader dialogue and efforts to manage this crisis, securing a better economic future for all.

As the situation unfolds, it's clear that resilience, creativity, and unity are more crucial than ever in ensuring that everyone in the UK can lead a fulfilling and less stressful life amidst these challenges.

Design

Design a poster to persuade people to donate food to the local food bank.

Keywords

Budget
An amount of money that you have available to spend.

Chancellor
The chancellor of the exchequer is the person responsible for how the government spends the country's money.

Cost of living
The cost of living is the amount of money that a person needs to buy food, clothing, heat their home or other basic things.

Debt
An amount of money that is owed by a person, company, country, etc.

Economy
The way in which a country manages its resources. References to the 'national economy' indicate the financial situation of a country: how wealthy or prosperous it is.

Inflation
A measure of the rate of rising prices of goods and services in an economy.

Interest rates
The cost of borrowing money. When money is borrowed, you need to pay back the amount borrowed *plus* the interest.

Means-Tested Benefits
If a benefit is means-tested, this means that your eligibility to claim it and how much money you receive will depend on your income and how much money in savings you have.

Recession
A period of time where there is a decline in economic activity.

Tax
An amount of money paid to the Government that is based on your income or the cost of goods or services you have bought.

300,000 more UK children fell into absolute poverty at height of cost-of-living crisis

Nearly a fifth of the population struggled with basic needs, it emerges, as charities accuse Government of failing poorest.

By Patrick Butler, Social policy editor

About 300,000 more children were plunged into absolute poverty in a single year at the height of the cost-of-living crisis amid soaring levels of hunger and food bank use, official figures show, prompting calls for an overhaul of the UK's creaking welfare safety net.

Campaigners accused the Government of failing to protect the UK's poorest families as the latest poverty statistics showed 600,000 more people fell into absolute poverty – ministers' preferred poverty measure – in 2022–23 when inflation was at its 10% peak.

Overall, during the year 12 million people were in absolute poverty – equivalent to 18% of the population, including 3.6 million children – levels of hardship last seen in 2011–12 after the financial crash.

Ministers and opposition politicians faced calls to get a grip on rising poverty levels, with charities urging an increase to benefit rates to reflect the real cost of basics, such as food and energy, and the scrapping of policies such as the two-child benefit limit which is seen as a driver of family hardship.

Campaigners said the meagreness of welfare benefits was highlighted by sharp rises in food insecurity and food bank use. One in 10 people in poverty relied on food banks during the year, while 41% of Universal Credit claimants were food insecure, meaning they could not afford to buy sufficient food.

The figures show the reality of increasing concerns over rising poverty, and the prevalence of more extreme forms of hardship such as destitution, where individuals are unable to afford basic living essentials such as food, energy, bedding and clothing. Nearly 4 million people experienced destitution in 2022.

The latest households below average income statistics, published by the Department for Work and Pensions, also showed that in 2022–23:

- More than two-thirds (69%) of UK children in poverty lived in families where at least one parent works, while 44% of children in lone-parent families were in poverty.

- An estimated 2.9 million children were in deep poverty, meaning their income was at least 50% below the poverty line. Nearly half (46%) of all families with three or more children were in poverty.

- Nearly one in 10 (8%) of pensioners struggled to eat regularly, pay essential bills or keep their home warm, up 2 percentage points year on year, and the first increase in material hardship measures among the over-65s since 2014.

Child poverty also increased on the relative poverty measure that is preferred by campaigners, with 100,000 more young people pulled beneath the poverty line, meaning that a third of UK children (4.3 million) were in poverty in 2022–23 on this calculation.

Alison Garnham, the chief executive of the Child Poverty Action Group, said: 'In a general election year, nothing should be more important to our political leaders than making things better for the country's poorest kids. But child poverty has reached a record high, with 4.3 million kids now facing cold homes and empty tummies.'

The Government said its cost-of-living support package, which included one-off cash payments and support with energy bills for low-income households, had helped alleviate pressure on poorer families and prevented more than 1 million people falling into poverty.

The work and pensions secretary, Mel Stride, acknowledged the 'last few years have been tough' but claimed falling inflation coupled with a range of tax and benefit measures would provide support to people on low incomes. 'The plan is working, and we need to stick to it to deliver a brighter future and economic security for everyone,' he said.

Charities said the second successive annual rise in absolute poverty figures showed it had failed to do enough. 'The government's short-term interventions to date haven't stopped the incomes of poorer households from being swallowed up by the soaring cost of essentials,' said Peter Matejic, the chief analyst at the Joseph Rowntree Foundation.

Labour called the figures 'horrifying' and promised to tackle the problem if it won power at the next election. Alison McGovern, the shadow welfare secretary, said: 'We'll fix this Tory failure yet again with a new cross-government child poverty strategy.'

But the party faced renewed calls to promise to scrap the Tories' two-child benefit limit, after the New Economics Foundation (NEF) thinktank highlighted that local authority areas in England with the biggest increases in child poverty in recent years also had high proportions of families affected by the two-child limit.

The three council areas of England with the largest rises in child poverty over the past decade (2014–15 to 2022–23), according to the NEF, were Nottingham (up 16 percentage points, with 40% of children in poverty), Birmingham (up 14 points, 41%) and Leicester (up 13 points, 41%).

Sam Tims, a senior economist at the NEF, said: 'What we are seeing is a deepening of poverty in the very places that the Government was supposed to lift up. The Government could take millions of children out of poverty and help those in the most deprived places by scrapping the two-child limit and increasing Universal Credit.'

Shona Goudie, a policy manager at the Food Foundation thinktank, said: 'Current benefit levels are clearly insufficient and hugely elevate risks of food insecurity and the health consequences of eating a poor diet.'

21 March 2024

Key facts

- In the year 2022–23, 12 million people were in absolute poverty, equivalent to 18% of the population, including 3.6 million children.
- In the same year, One in 10 people in poverty relied on food banks.
- 41% of Universal Credit claimants were food insecure, meaning they could not afford to buy sufficient food.
- Nearly 4 million people experienced destitution in 2022.
- 69% of UK children in poverty lived in families where at least one parent works.
- 44% of children in lone-parent families were in poverty.
- Roughly 2.9 million children were in deep poverty, meaning their income was at least 50% below the poverty line.
- 46% of all families with three or more children were in poverty.
- Nearly one in 10 (8%) of pensioners struggled to eat regularly, pay essential bills or keep their home warm.
- The three council areas of England with the largest rises in child poverty over the past decade (2014-15 to 2022-23), according to the NEF, were Nottingham (up 16 percentage points, with 40% of children in poverty), Birmingham (up 14 points, 41%) and Leicester (up 13 points, 41%).

Design

Design a poster on poverty in the UK, highlighting facts, personal stories (fictional or real-life case studies), and possible solutions to help people understand the crisis.

The above information is reprinted with kind permission from The Guardian.
© 2024 Guardian News and Media Limited

www.theguardian.com

The cost-of-living conundrum

Why falling inflation isn't ending the crisis.

By Tom Clark

Last week, we learned that inflation had been safely steered back to 2%, precisely in line with the Bank of England target. Everything, then, is back under control. We can safely draw a line under the 'cost-of-living crisis'. Right? Sadly, nothing could be further from the truth.

What matters for securing the absolute basics in life – food, shelter, heat and so on – is not a general price level (which is also affected by the prices of luxury holidays, fancy restaurants and the bill for domestic staff) but the costs of those very necessities. The rise in private rents is sharp and ongoing; they continue to climb not by 2%, but nearly 9% a year. Energy bills may now be falling, but from such a ludicrous peak that they are still up around 60% on three years ago. Food, meanwhile, is up by around 30% over the same period.

Set all this against what's happened to incomes at the bottom end of the scale, and the gap is stark. For poorer families, benefits are a source of income, and for the very poorest often the only source of income. When, after an extremely painful delay, headline benefit rates finally caught up with general inflation in April this year, the rise over the period from April 2021 was merely 20% – far lower than the increase in the price of food, shelter or fuel. So keeping body and soul together is still a good deal more difficult than it used to be: the cost-of-surviving crisis continues.

And yet the very idea of a cost-of-living 'crisis' was, arguably, always a misnomer. It is the nature of crises to culminate in a particular moment, but the hardship laid bare in the last couple of years always had less to do with a passing inflationary moment than a stubborn – and enduring – squeeze on the lowest incomes. In medical terms, we are not dealing with an acute emergency, but the sort of chronic condition that has long dogged, and shortened, life in large parts of the United States.

Let's recall a few facts. Rough sleeping in England is up by 60% over the last two years, and the number of families stuck in (reliably terrible) temporary accommodation has doubled since 2010. Government statisticians have recently started publishing data on food banks; this plank of the survival system of poorer people has simply become too big for them to ignore. The official tally of people whose households had turned to food banks in the last 12 months stands at 2.3 million. In the same statisticians' numbing bureaucratic parlance, 'very low food security' now stands at 3.7 million, a total that has shot up by a full two-thirds in the latest year alone. These numbers are on the same scale as the notorious 'three million unemployed' which was seen as the defining blight on British society in the 1980s. Our unfolding decade deserves to be damned as 'the Hungry Twenties.'

The consequences of all this hardship for broader society have become increasingly stark over the past year. Both official and retail industry figures are recording an astonishing surge in shoplifting, something industry insiders have linked to a black market for food that has burgeoned during the big squeeze. Still darker indicators flash in relation to health. British progress on longevity has been faltering for a while, but in the last couple of years things have gone into outright reverse. According to the Office for National Statistics, life expectancy at birth for 2020/22 is 'back to the same level as

2010/12 for females' and 'slightly below' that benchmark for males – a whole decade, in other words, of zero or negative progress.

This isn't normal. Barring war or revolutionary convulsions, lives have always got longer, not shorter, in industrial societies. Admittedly, the pandemic colours the recent picture, but the slide started earlier. Even before the virus, we saw women specifically in poorer postcodes beginning to die earlier. Then, when Covid-19 came, the (mostly male) deaths it caused piled up disproportionately in the same poor neighbourhoods. Moreover, the perennial inequality in healthy life expectancy has grown. 'The most deprived areas of England,' government demographers report, registered 'a significant decrease' on this count in the second half of the 2010s. Looking ahead to 2040 (and comparing against a 2019 baseline), analysts at Liverpool University and the Health Foundation foresee an increase of some 700,000 in the number of working-age Britons living with a major long-term illness, overwhelmingly accounted for by a further rocketing of already-heavy rates of chronic pain, diabetes and anxiety/depression in poorer communities. Irrespective of any moral concern about poverty, or indeed basic humanity, purely in terms of employment and productivity that sounds like a very expensive problem in the making.

Will a new, in all likelihood Labour, government make much difference? In some ways, it might well. Under its banner of 'securonomics', Labour will substantially further the now well-established cross-party tide towards stronger interventions in poverty-inducing markets. George Osborne, remember, started the recent process of ramping up the minimum wage the Tories once opposed; Theresa May commissioned the Taylor review to explore insecurities in the gig economy; Michael Gove tried (and ultimately failed) to banish no-fault evictions; and, Liz Truss (of all people) introduced an energy price guarantee.

Keir Starmer will go further on most of these fronts. Labour would, for example, not just talk about banning no-fault evictions, but actually do so. And, even if it shrinks from that outright ban on zero-hour contracts (for which there is a powerful argument), the party is firmly committed to meaningfully strengthening worker protections against the vicissitudes of unreliable shifts. If it can do all this and also engineer the stronger economic growth it promises, then the 'working people' it talks endlessly about will be more in demand and in a stronger negotiating position to push for further improvements of terms and conditions.

What's much less clear, however, is whether Labour will reinforce the original and surest form of 'securonomics' – namely, social security. I recently wrote about the party's failure to challenge the government's dehumanising two-child policy and while it has since been a relief to hear Starmer half-acknowledging the force of the argument for scrapping it, he's still a long way off from committing to action. The truth is that this is only the most grievous of the many holes that years of austerity have torn in the social safety net. Rates of basic benefits are now lower relative to wages than at any time since the inception of the Beveridge settlement, which established the welfare state in the 1940s. Basic protection against unemployment in the UK are also the lowest in the OECD.

Without adequate basic benefits, millions of Britons are standing on a trapdoor to poverty; it only takes a redundancy, injury or divorce for them to fall through it. This is the single most important cause of the hardship so evident across the country. And yet, hopes of addressing it now rest on a single line in the Starmer manifesto: 'Labour is committed to reviewing Universal Credit so that it makes work pay and tackles poverty.'

It is hardly a transformational promise. But if the political will is there, a review could open the door to meaningful change. Last year I held the pen on the Resolution Foundation's strategy for ending stagnation, which explained in detail how, with even moderate growth, UK demographics leave plenty of scope for steadily raising working-age benefits back towards reasonable levels without increasing the burden of welfare on the economy. It is time to banish the lie that basic decency is a luxury we can no longer afford.

We can discuss different elements of deprivation – cold, squalor, hunger and so on – and debate different elements of the solution. In the end, however, we are talking about one problem: a marauding giant of Want runs across the entire terrain. The biggest question for our generation, as for William Beveridge and the generation that came through the war, is once again how to summon the political will in order to slay it.

25 June 2024

Define

Write a one-paragraph definition of the following words:
- Cost-of-living
- Poverty
- Inflation

Research

Who was William Beveridge? Find out some information about him and what he did and write a short biography.

The above information is reprinted with kind permission from *Prospect Magazine*.
© 2024 Prospect Publishing Limited

www.prospectmagazine.co.uk

What the cost-of-living crisis looks like around the world

While the global economy is predicted to have a 'soft landing', countries like Sudan are facing a cost-of-living catastrophe.

The 'cost-of-living crisis' is now a familiar phrase as prices of everyday goods have increased dramatically in recent years. In the UK, prices remain high while consumer prices have been increasing around the world, too, with average global inflation at 6.8% in 2023. This means that food, energy bills, and rent are still getting more expensive for everyone.

But while the global economy is forecast for a 'soft landing' in 2024, countries where the International Rescue Committee (IRC) works, like Sudan, are facing a cost-of-living catastrophe on a whole different scale.

A year since conflict began in Sudan, the economy is on the brink of collapse, and spiralling prices for food and basic necessities are further contributing to the world's worst humanitarian crisis.

Sudan's cost-of-living catastrophe

Sudan is currently at the top of the IRC's Emergency Watchlist for 2024. After one year of fighting, the country is experiencing the world's worst displacement crisis and one of the world's worst hunger crises. Humanitarian needs have more than doubled since the start of the conflict, with nearly 25 million people in need of help.

Food prices are a significant problem within the wider crisis. A new report published by the IRC found that, while markets are stocked with food in many areas, people cannot afford to buy goods due to higher prices. Food prices have increased by 88% since the war began – even in areas not directly affected by the conflict – and were already soaring before the war with inflation reaching 359.1% in 2021.

Ali was forced to flee Sudan with his family. The conflict and economic situation meant their only option was to leave their lives behind, including the family business. 'This war has affected me emotionally, financially, in every way,' he said, speaking to International Rescue Committee staff at a transit centre in neighbouring South Sudan.

People in Sudan urgently need cash assistance

Sudan is quickly becoming the world's largest hunger crisis and emergency cash transfers offer a crucial lifeline. A report by the IRC and regional partners found that while markets are well-stocked with food and goods, people are unable to afford them due to rapidly rising prices.

Afghanistan's cost-of-living crisis

Since the shift in power in Afghanistan in August 2021, the country has experienced near economic collapse. Policies meant to isolate the Taliban by cutting off Afghanistan from the international financial system have crippled the national economy.

Ordinary Afghans have paid the price of economic crisis that left millions of people without a source of income. People who had jobs and were self-sufficient are now relying on humanitarian aid. Poverty is extremely high across the country, with nearly 50% of Afghan households struggling to meet basic needs.

Noor* fled Kunduz Province with her three children when the Taliban came and conflict was raging. She had no time to bring any belongings except some clothes for her kids.

'I thank [the IRC] for what they have done for us so far,' she said after she received cash assistance in late 2021. 'Today, I want to buy tea and sugar, onions, and things like that we need. It means that my kids will not starve to death. Now, they are hopeful.'

The IRC in Afghanistan

In 2022, the IRC scaled up our staff in Afghanistan from 1,700 to 5,000 today, with 99% Afghan staff, and 40% of staff who are women. We operate in 12 provinces, supporting 68 health facilities and running 30 mobile health teams across the country. We also provide emergency cash assistance, family support centres, and employment skills training.

Lebanon's cost-of-living crisis

One of the most severe inflation crises recorded has led to economic collapse in Lebanon, with an increasing number of people being unable to afford their cost-of-living. The economic turmoil in Lebanon also impacts the 1.5 million Syrian refugees who have found safety in the country. Across the country, both Lebanese and refugees are now struggling to afford their basic costs.

Since 2019, Lebanon's GDP has shrunk 40% while consumer prices continue to soar, reaching inflation rates of 170% for the year 2022. Prices of goods have risen while the value of wages has fallen, forcing consumers to turn to importers who sell crucial goods, like fuel and medicine, on the black market.

The IRC in Lebanon

Since 2012, the IRC has been providing legal services, education, cash assistance, training and economic support for refugees and local communities.

Somalia's cost-of-living crisis

Somalia's economic outlook has been hampered by a series of shocks that have left its people struggling to afford basic necessities. A series of climate-induced disasters and ongoing political unrest have left Somalis with an extreme cost-of-living crisis.

Somalia's recent drought has been the longest and most severe in four decades, and its effects are expected to be felt long after. The drought has impacted food supplies, with 4.3 million people facing crisis (or worse) levels of food insecurity.

Following the drought, heavy seasonal rains caused catastrophic flooding in late 2023 which destroyed farmland and forced more than 706,000 people from their homes. Damage from flooding could lead to reduced farming production and a higher risk of crop failures, driving decreased household purchasing power and high food costs at markets.

The IRC in Somalia

The IRC is scaling up our programs in Somalia to address drought and rising food insecurity. We provide health, nutrition, water and sanitation services; women's protection and empowerment; and cash assistance to drought-affected populations across the country.

Names have been changed for client privacy

25 April 2024

Did you know?

The International Rescue Committee (IRC) works in more than 40 countries and over 29 US cities to help people affected by humanitarian crises to survive, recover and rebuild their lives.

The International Rescue Committee responds to the world's worst humanitarian crises, including the conflict in Ukraine and the crisis in Gaza. We help to restore health, safety, education, economic wellbeing and power to people devastated by conflict and disaster. And we are proud to fight for a world where women and girls have an equal chance to succeed.

Visit www.rescue.org to find out more...

The above information is reprinted with kind permission from International Rescue Committee, UK.
© International Rescue Committee 2024

www.rescue.org

'People buy spectacularly less': inflation-hit Europe weighs costs ahead of elections

Governments have tried to ease the pain from record-high inflation that has swept Europe. But they failed to tame a major inflation driver in corporate 'greedflation'. Now European elections approach with the cost-of-living crisis high on agendas.

By Pascal Hansens and Attila Kálmán

On paper, Europe's inflation crisis is easing. Rates have dropped from double digit highs of 2022, and the OECD said in May that inflation was 'falling faster than initially projected and private sector confidence is improving'. Yet for the European public, inflation's impact remains very real. 'I used to buy feta for €7–8 per kilo, now it's €14. Of course I don't buy it at that price, I hunt for special offers and go to several supermarkets every week,' says Maria, 63, who works as a cleaner in Athens. She says many Greeks have changed shopping habits because of high inflation and now must shop around the city searching for bargains.

On the other side of Europe, Frédéric, who lives near Paris, is also hit by high prices. 'It's quite simple, my gas and electricity bills have clearly risen by an easy 35%'. The French accountant has started keeping track of his expenses in a spreadsheet to see where his money is going, and he sees that food and utilities have jumped the most.

The situation in the middle of the continent is even worse. 'People are buying spectacularly less and yet paying more. Many people are nervous and tense when they have to pay, some even swear,' said Réka, a supermarket cashier in Budapest. No wonder, Hungary has the highest food inflation in Europe, with prices almost doubling since 2020.

Annual inflation across the EU reached a record-high of 11.5% in October 2022 (the European Central Bank sets a two% target). Spiralling prices were triggered by the fallout from the Covid-19 pandemic, the destabilising impact of Russia's invasion of Ukraine and flawed national policy-making. What's more, many prices have spiked further due to unchecked corporate 'greedflation' tactics.

It is of little surprise, then, that poverty and the cost-of-living crisis are priorities for voters in June's European elections, according to a Eurobarometer survey. Millions remain gripped by concerns about housing, jobs and daily expenses and far-right parties are among those targeting such fears on the campaign trail. Jordan Bardella, candidate for the far-right Rassemblement National, has said purchasing power is 'one of the great untreated anguishes' of citizens. 'Inflation is a wall in front of which millions of French people ... can no longer cope.'

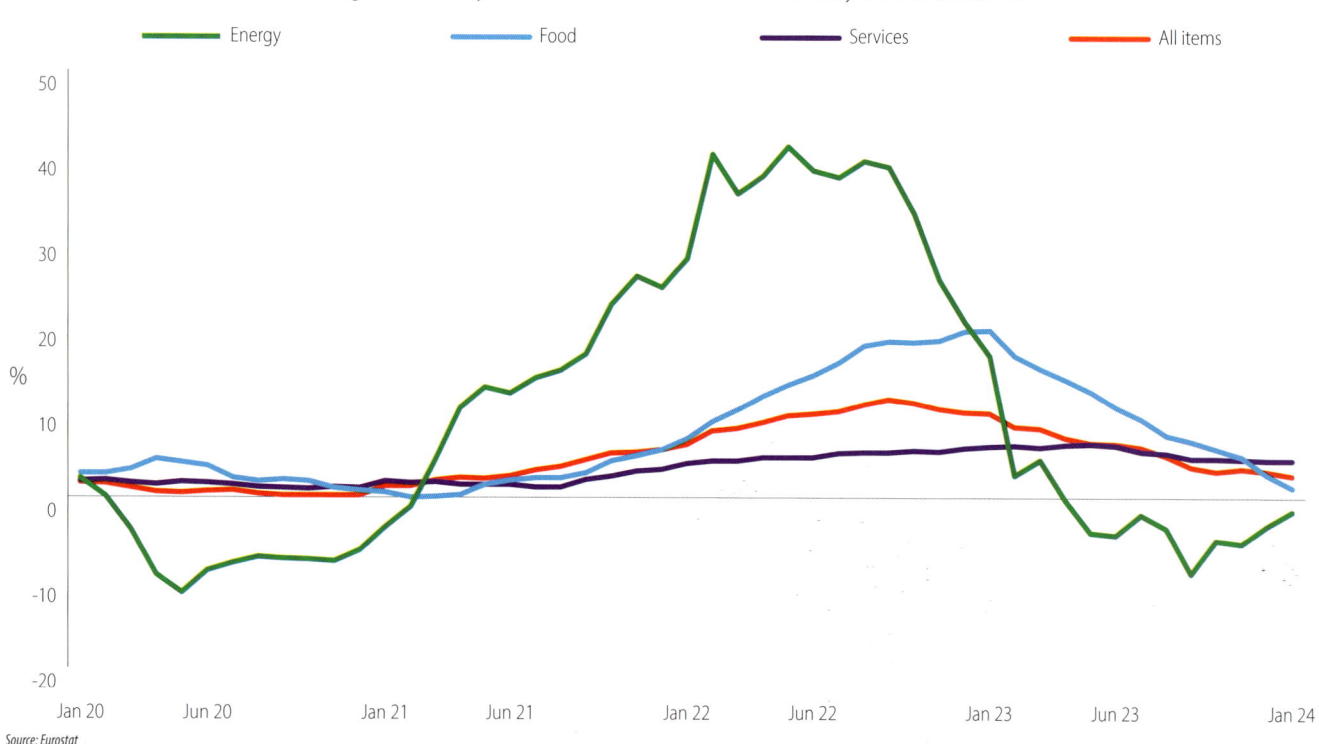

Food and energy prices soar in Europe after Covid-19 pandemic and Ukraine invasion
Changes in monthly inflation rates in the EU27 from January 2020 to March 2024

Source: Eurostat

After the Russian invasion, inflation was mainly fuelled by soaring energy costs, but by early 2023 Europe had adapted to its new energy supply. Food prices had become the main cause of inflation. And now we have reached the point where the rise in the cost of services is the leading cause. As András, a hairdresser in Budapest, puts it: 'The landlord raised the salon rent at the beginning of the year with the official inflation figure, so that's why I'm raising the price.'

Not surprisingly, countries more dependent on Russian gas have seen the biggest increases in energy prices in recent years. At the same time, wages have not risen at a similar rate. Only Belgium (2.9%) - where wages are fully indexed on inflation - and the Netherlands (0.4%) saw real hourly wages rise between the first quarters of 2022 and 2023. The fall in real wages ranged from 0.8% in Luxembourg to 15.6% in Hungary.

There are many reasons for this. A significant one is the lack of coverage of workers by collective agreements, according to Nicolas Schmit, the European Commissioner for Jobs and Social Rights. A recently-adopted European directive sets a non-binding target of 80% coverage. Schmit, who is running for the EU Commission presidency in June, believes that wage indexation, as in Belgium and Luxembourg, could be a solution but it has its limits.

> 'I used to buy feta for €7–8 per kilo, now it's €14. Of course I don't buy it at that price, I hunt for special offers.' – Maria, 63, Athens

In January 2023, Spain reduced VAT on staple foods from 4% to zero in an attempt to address its inflation crisis. This was a move that several governments have tried to do, including the Polish, Italian and Portuguese. Another common measure to combat food inflation was the introduction of price caps, which Hungary took advantage of. Not with much success, because the supermarkets recouped the lost profits on artificially low-priced products by mark-ups on other products.

The Greek Government found a third way. On supermarket prices, one of the most successful measures against inflation was the three-month ban on sales promotion of goods that recently had a price hike. Companies renounced on price increases out of fear that they would lose market share.

With gas and oil prices spiralling out of control, almost all governments have also regulated fuel prices: sometimes with price caps (Hungary again), sometimes with rebates (Germany, Spain), sometimes with VAT cuts (Italy, Poland).

While keeping fuel prices under control has helped both households and companies, subsidising energy prices has essentially only affected households, with full prices

An increasing number of Europeans can't afford to heat their homes
Percentage of population unable to heat their homes adequately in selected EU27 countries, in **2020** and **2022**.

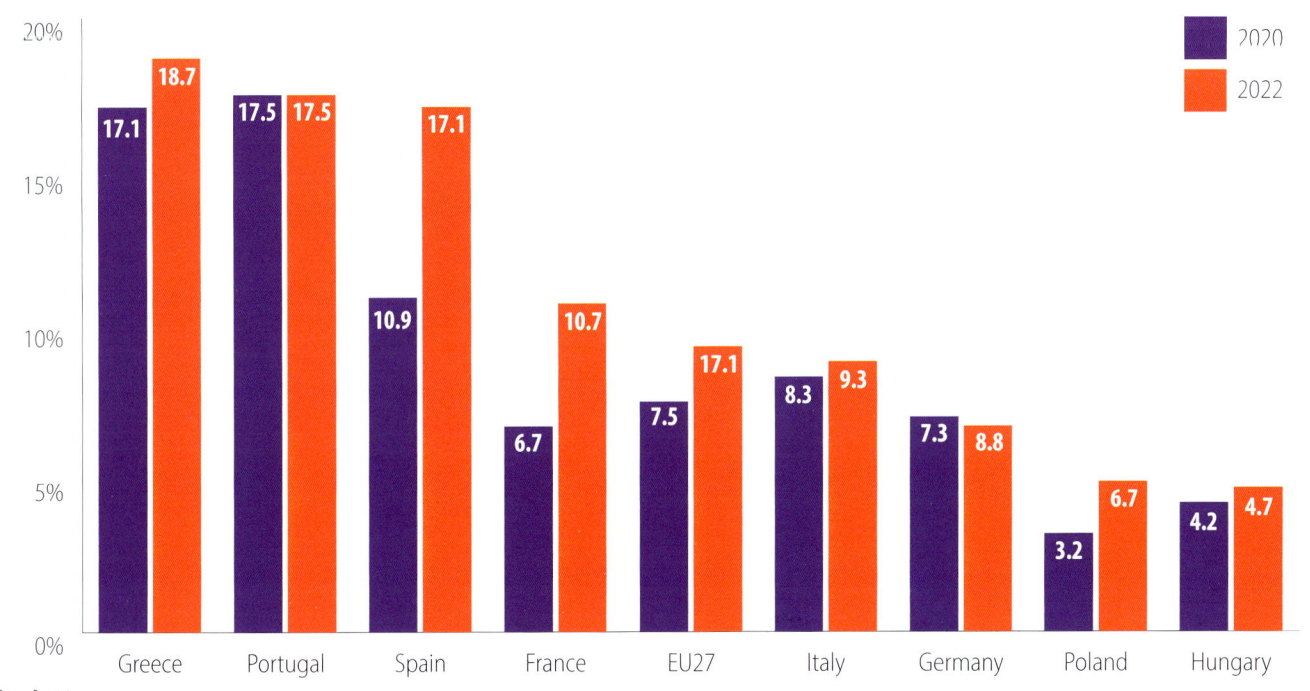

Source: Eurostat

in place above a certain consumption. For businesses and entrepreneurs in need of large amounts of energy, this has been the biggest problem and has fuelled inflation. On the other hand, it left the most money in people's pockets, but it really cost governments a lot.

Inflation always hits the poorest hardest. Portugal and Italy have offered one-off subsidies to help the least well off, but they are in the minority. The bleak reality is illustrated by how many people are now unable to heat their homes. Since 2021, the picture has worsened dramatically in most of Europe.

In Spain and Greece one in five people cannot meet their basic utility needs. 'The other problem you have in Greece and in the European Union is that inflation is higher for those who have lower incomes,' says Greek MEP Georgios Kyrtsos. 'Because they spend all their money on housing, energy and food.'

But the last two years were not bad for everyone. Many corporations and their shareholders thrived. France's top companies, comprising the CAC 40 index, celebrated a record-breaking year in 2023, with combined profits of €153.6 billion. According to the European Trade Union Confederation (ETUC), profit share increased across the EU by 4% since the start of the Covid-19 pandemic. Dividend payments to shareholders rose up to 13 times faster than wages.

This can be partly explained by a blind spot in the measures deployed to combat inflation, namely the fight against 'greedflation', where companies exploit inflation to justify exorbitant price hikes, prioritising profit over consumer welfare. It can occur when companies anticipate increased production costs, and so they artificially raise consumer prices. Or when higher retail prices remain in place even if production costs come down again.

'Europe's businesses have so far been shielded more than workers from the adverse cost shock.' – International Monetary Fund

Already last June, European Central Bank President Christine Lagarde sounded the alarm. She emphasised how certain sectors had capitalised on supply-demand imbalances and volatile inflation to boost profits. She pointed to the agriculture, construction and service industries for potential unjustified price increases, urging competition authorities to scrutinise the practices.

In the eurozone, recent inflation largely stems from higher profits and import prices. Profits contributed to 45% of price hikes since early 2022, according to a briefing last June by the International Monetary Fund. 'Europe's businesses have so far been shielded more than workers from the adverse cost shock,' the authors assessed.

Greedflation is much stronger than wage-induced inflation, says French economist Jézabel Couppey-Soubeyran, for whom this phenomenon is also due to market concentration, which is an underlying trend, particularly in the energy, food, and banking sectors. 'What we have seen in recent years is companies, particularly in the retail sector, passing on price rises in their selling prices. It's this problem that we need to take into account and try to limit. Member States have not really got to grips with the problem.'

French President Emmanuel Macron last year attacked the 'cynicism' of those 'who make such exceptional income that they end up using this money to buy back their own shares'. He promised to implement a tax so that 'workers can benefit' from the outsized returns. Greek Prime Minister Kyriakos Mitsotakis also denounced 'greedflation', telling companies that Greece 'is not a banana republic'.

But concrete action has rarely followed, and monitoring mechanisms are still inadequate. Investigate Europe analysis of national policies found no clear steps taken to curb the

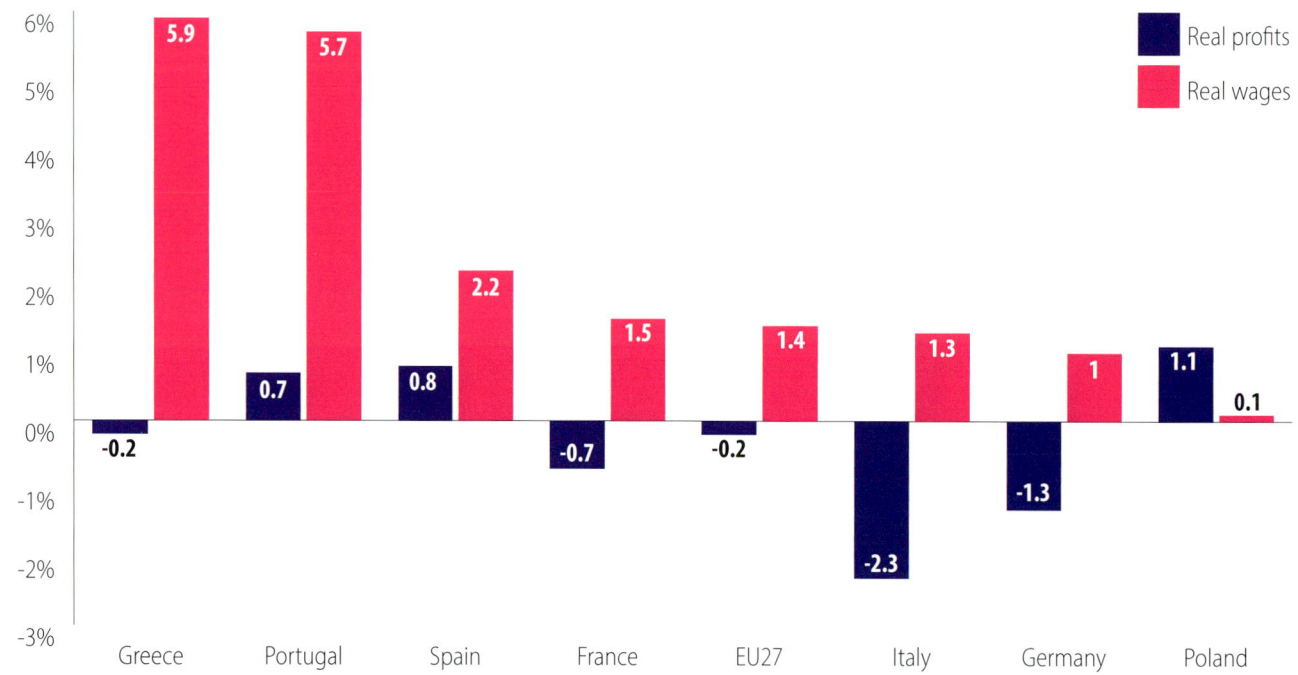

Inflated gains: corporate profits rise as wages stagnate
Growth rates in real wages and real profits in selected EU27 countries in 2023

Source: European Trade Union Confederation, European Commission database

phenomenon, except in the energy sector. Back in 2022, the EU adopted an emergency regulation to address high energy prices, setting a mandatory temporary solidarity contribution on the surplus of fossil fuel businesses. But this ended in December 2023.

The contribution of profit to inflation 'had gone a little bit missing,' the ECB President lamented to European parliamentarians. The reason, she said, is simple: 'We don't have as much and as good data on profit as we do on wages.'

There is no shared acceptance among political players that greedflation has strongly impacted everyone, says Ester Lynch, general secretary of the ETUC. 'I think the political persuasion and who governments listen to may explain this governmental inappetence to act against excess profits,' she says. 'There wasn't that same acceptance that, by driving up prices, profit increases affected everybody. On the workers' side, we were adamant and pushing but there wasn't the same sense of urgency from governments.'

EU Commissioner Schmit cautions against oversimplifying the issue. But he thinks corporations should pay their fair share and pay taxes on super profits to invest in the green transition and defence industries: 'We are talking about thousands of billions of euros if we take the figures for the next 10 years.'

> 'If we don't fight against the structural part ... climate change and fossil fuel phase-out, we're going to remain exposed to price volatility.' – Jézabel Couppey-Soubeyran

Currently, there's a positive outlook: inflation has tapered off to around 2% from its 2022 high, largely due to declines in energy and food prices. 'The impact of tighter monetary conditions continues ... but global activity is proving relatively resilient, inflation is falling faster than initially projected and private sector confidence is improving,' an OECD report released in May assessed. However, profits need to fall further if inflation is to remain around the 2% target, the European Central Bank said in an April analysis.

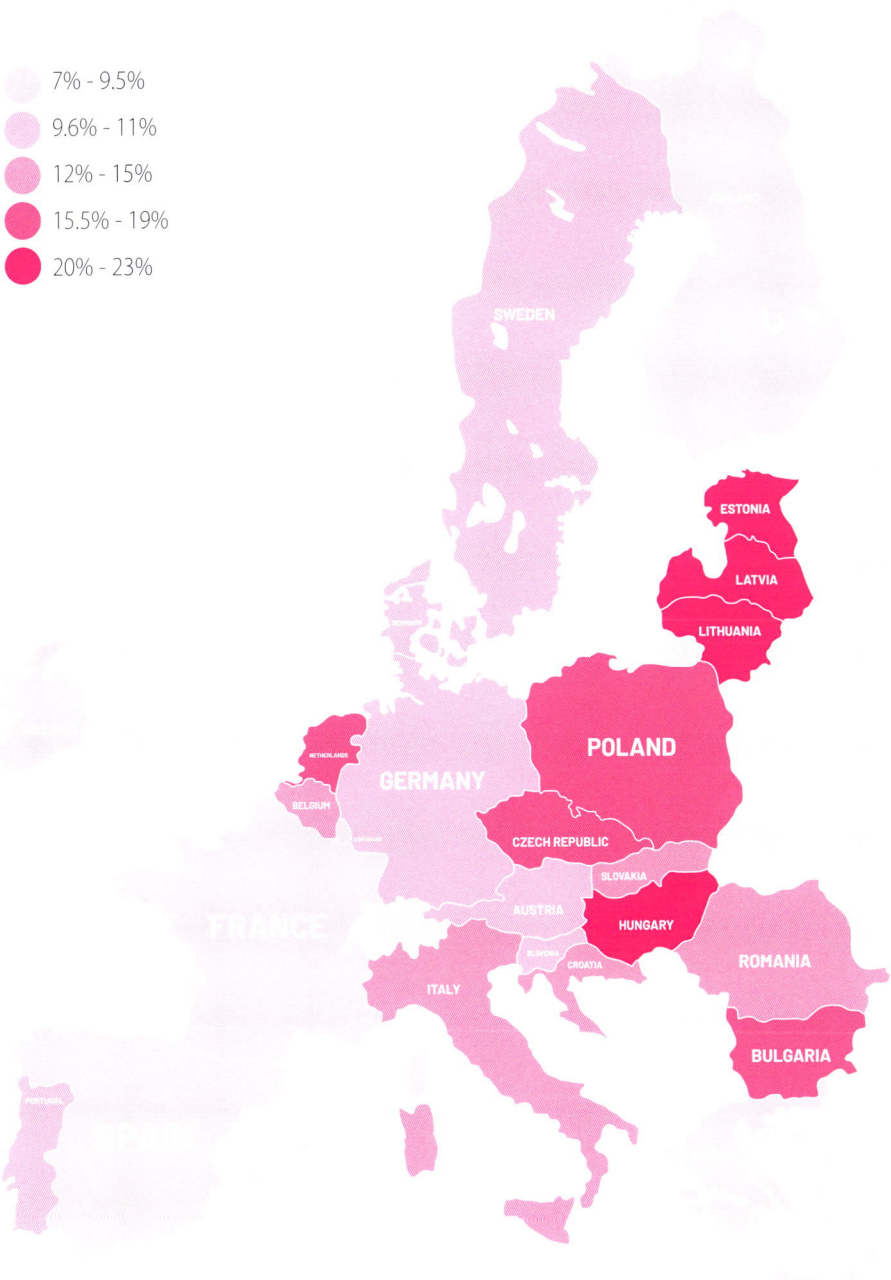

Hungary and the Baltic countries hit hardest by inflation
EU27 inflation rate in October 2022, the highest month on record since 2020.

- 7% - 9.5%
- 9.6% - 11%
- 12% - 15%
- 15.5% - 19%
- 20% - 23%

Source: Eurostat

But another storm will come. Economist Jézabel Couppey-Soubeyran suggests that while inflation appears to be stabilising, it is premature to declare it over. 'If we don't fight against the structural part, namely against climate change and fossil fuel phase-out, we're going to remain exposed to price volatility,' she says.

The European Parliament in December voted on whether to support a temporary crisis solidarity tax on 'undue and excessive profits'. The resolution narrowly failed – 282 votes in favour and 300 against. Opposition came mostly from conservatives and the far-right – the same parties tipped for major gains in June's elections.

16 May 2024

The above information is reprinted with kind permission from Investigate Europe.
© 2024 Investigate Europe

www.investigate-europe.eu

How the cost-of-living crisis affects young people around the world

By Douglas Broom

- Younger workers have been hit hard by the rising cost-of-living, according to a new survey.
- Gen Z and millennials are losing hope of owning their own homes and even starting a family.
- Recent research concludes we need better jobs and opportunities for all.

The world is suffering a cost-of-living crisis as inflation has surged and disposable incomes have been squeezed. The full impact on young adults has been highlighted by a new survey.

Consultants Deloitte polled 22,000 Gen Z and millennial respondents in 44 nations about the effect of soaring prices on their lives and found that the cost-of-living was the number one concern for both groups, ahead of worries about losing their jobs, climate change and mental health.

Deloitte's 2023 Millennial and Gen Z Survey is the 12th annual snapshot of the lives of Generation Z (Gen Z) – people born between January 1995 and December 2004 – and millennials – people born between January 1983 and December 1994.

The study found that many were feeling the financial squeeze so acutely they had taken second jobs to help make ends meet and were pessimistic about their ability to enjoy benefits taken for granted by previous generations, like homes and families.

One young woman from New Zealand summed up the feelings of many when she told the survey: 'I'm unable to afford to start a family and have had to take on a second job, which is affecting my health.'

Hardest on the young

The World Economic Forum's Future of Jobs 2023 report says the economic fallout from the Covid-19 pandemic has 'disproportionately impacted young workers', urging business and political leaders to invest to create better jobs and opportunities for all.

Since the pandemic and Russia's invasion of Ukraine, inflation has surged, particularly for food, which has seen

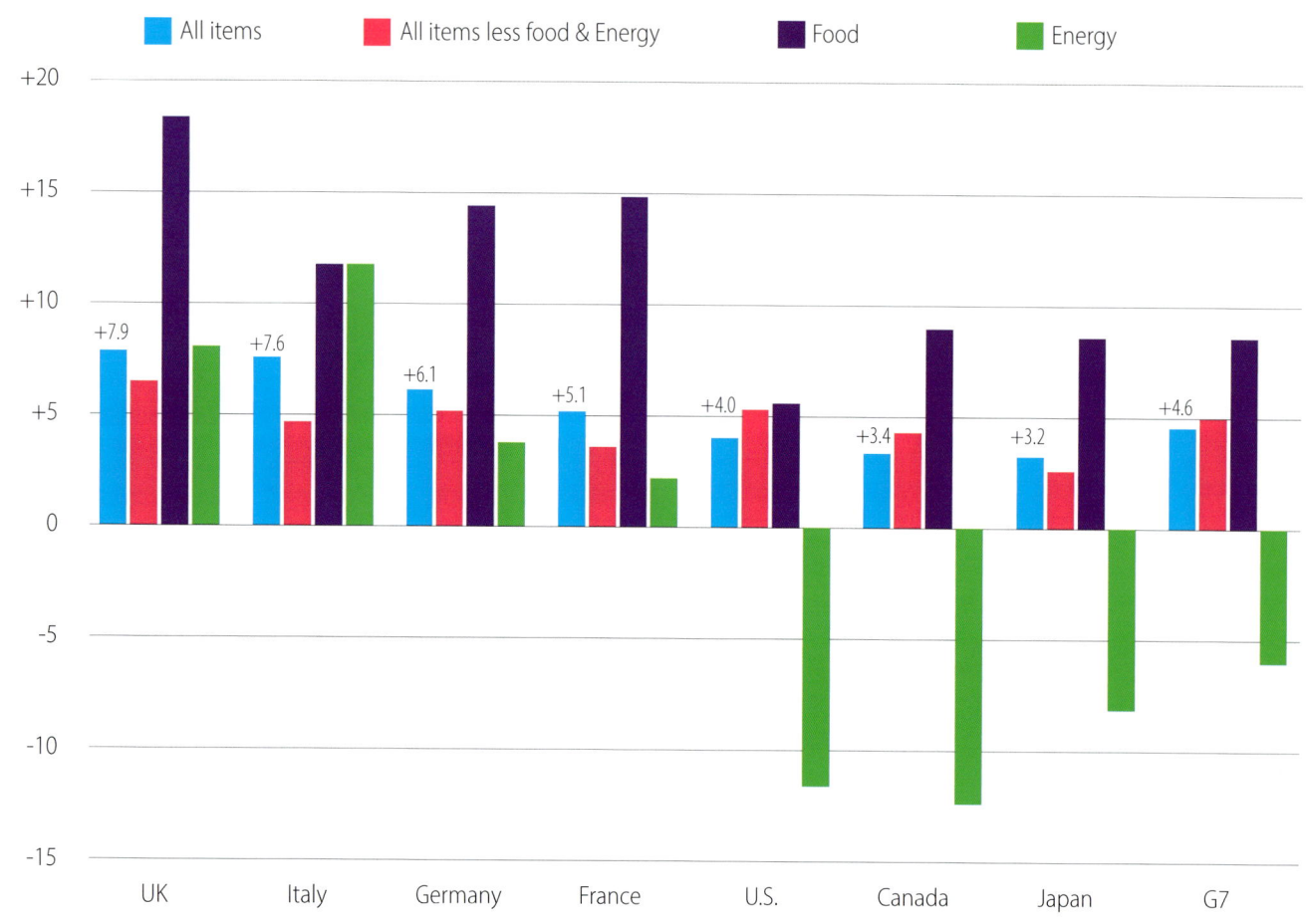

Which G7 economies have the highest inflation?
Inflation rates in G7 countries in May 2023 (in %)

Source: Statista

Top drivers for taking on a side job:
- Gen Zs
- Millennials
- I needed a secondary source of income
- It helps me to develop important skills and relationships
- It is a hobby of mine
- It helps me to turn off/focus on something other than my main job

Source: Deloitte

price increases outstripping other commodities. In the worst affected countries, the price of food rose by triple-digit percentages, according to World Bank data.

Inflation is still high in many developed countries

Asked by Deloitte about the sources of stress in their lives, young people cited worries about their longer-term financial futures, day-to-day finances and the health and welfare of their families.

'The cost-of-living is getting higher and higher. I have concerns about not being able to pay my bills and not giving my children the education and life they deserve,' a woman from Brazil added.

One Gen Z man put it like this: 'My main financial concern will be ensuring I can have a comfortable work-life balance, as at present I am struggling to maintain this due to picking up a lot of overtime to make ends meet.'

A third of those surveyed fear that if the current economic climate persists it will become harder to ask for more flexibility at work to improve their work-life balance and 15% think it will become impossible.

More than half of both millennials and Gen Zs think the current financial situation makes it impossible to ask for a raise or a promotion. Even so, the quarter of Gen Z and 13% of millennials who plan to quit in the next year say pay is the top reason for changing jobs.

Money was cited as the main reason for taking on a second job, with 46% of millennials and 38% of Gen Z saying they needed extra work to stay afloat. The most popular second jobs were selling online and gig work, such as for food delivery or ride-sharing apps.

Changing behaviour

As well as second jobs, young people are also changing their behaviour to save money, according to Deloitte, with popular steps including shunning fast fashion and buying second-hand clothes, not driving a car and switching to vegetarian or vegan diets.

Almost two-thirds believe owning their own home will be harder or even impossible in the future, and half of Gen Z and 47% of millennials say starting a family is going to be out of reach or very hard.

Over half of both groups say they exist from one payday to the next with no margin, an increase of five percentage points on the previous survey in 2022. However, two-fifths of Gen Z and a third of millennials expect their financial situation to improve over the next year.

While online and digital media has provided new sources of income for some, it's also become a source of financial anxiety for others, the survey found. Over half of Gen Z and 43% of millennials say social media makes them want to buy things they can't afford.

The cost-of-living crisis is also testing their commitment to shopping sustainably. Six in 10 of both generations say they are willing to pay more for sustainable products and services, but more than half say they won't be able to afford to if the economic situation does not improve.

8 August 2023

The above information is reprinted with kind permission from World Economic Forum.
© 2024 World Economic Forum

www.weforum.org

Is the cost-of-living crisis over and will prices in the UK ever come down?

What does the inflation rate mean for you? Will prices come down? Here's what you need to know about whether the cost-of-living crisis will ever end

By Isabella Mcrae

It feels like the cost-of-living crisis has lasted an age. Although inflation has now reached 'normal' levels, we have faced prices rising at rates not seen in decades while wages struggled to keep up. So is the cost-of-living crisis nearly over, and will prices ever come down?

Inflation fell to 2% in the year to May 2024, down from 2.3% the month before. That's the lowest level in nearly three years, and means inflation has finally hit the Bank of England's 2% target.

Food and non-alcoholic drink prices are up by 1.7% on last year, finally below the headline rate of inflation.

But lower inflation rate doesn't mean prices are falling – in fact, they are still rising, just at a slower rate.

People are still feeling the impact of the cost-of-living crisis. Families are struggling with debt and many have spent far too long sacrificing essentials with nothing left.

So, what does inflation actually mean for you? We break down everything you need to know about whether the cost-of-living crisis is ever actually going to come to an end.

What actually is inflation? And what does it mean for me?

The term 'inflation' is the technical way of describing the rate at which prices are rising. But what does it actually mean and how does it impact your life? If you've noticed the cost of a bunch of bananas or a pack of loo rolls is still getting more expensive and your household bills keep on soaring, that's because inflation was high for, well, far too long. The higher the inflation rate, the faster your bills increase.

The inflation rate of 2% in May 2024 means prices have risen by 2% on average in comparison to May 2023. Prices are still increasing and will continue to as long as inflation is in positive figures.

If you want to see just how much more expensive your shopping basket is going to be as a result of inflation, you could use a price comparison website like Trolley. It has a grocery price index with data showing how much all your basic supermarket items have increased in recent months.

Will prices in the UK ever come down?

The simple answer is that UK prices across the board will probably never come down – and almost certainly not by very much – but wages are supposed to keep up with rising prices to make us less likely to feel the pinch.

For prices in the UK to fall, inflation would need to go into negative figures, often called deflation. That is a rarity. The last time this happened was in 2015 when prices fell by a grand total of 0.1% because of a sudden drop in the price of oil.

Before that was in 2009, during the global financial crisis, but economists disagree on the details as only one measure of prices was negative. You have to go back to 1960 to find another example of deflation.

But don't panic. The cost-of-living crisis will come to an end eventually. Prices will stabilise and grow more slowly and real wages should catch up, with progress being made on this already.

When will the cost-of-living crisis end?

The cost-of-living crisis will be over once prices stabilise and wages have risen enough to match. With wage growth above inflation, the cost-of-living crisis 'appears to be coming to an end'.

Recent ONS data shows that annual earnings growth, excluding bonuses, was 6% in the three months up to April 2024 in comparison to the previous year. After taking inflation into account, real pay growth was 2.3%, so we should be feeling slightly better off.

But the problem is, most people have already faced a large drop in living standards. The financial year 2022 to 2023 was the largest year-on-year drop in living standards since ONS records began in the 1950s – and it will take time to recover from that.

The Office for Budget Responsibility (OBR) predicts that living standards will grow by around 1% a year on average, and should recover to their pre-pandemic peak by 2025–2026, two years earlier than they had previously predicted.

Around 90% of Brits believe that the cost-of-living crisis is still ongoing, according to recent polling from campaign group Stop the Squeeze, and campaigners warn that the 'real damage has already been done'.

Megan Davies from Stop the Squeeze said: 'Lower inflation doesn't mean the cost-of-living crisis is over, in fact for many families things are going to get worse rather than better.

'It's no use telling people the economy is booming when they are close to going bust, declaring job done will only fuel the sense that the government doesn't understand how squeezed people are feeling.

'Instead of a victory lap, we need a real cost-of-living plan for Britain, focused on addressing the root causes of the crisis and getting people's incomes up and their bills down.'

Real wages are still worth less today than in 2008. The Trades Union Congress (TUC) estimates that, had wages grown at their pre-crisis trend, the average worker would be over £14,000 a year better off.

The TUC has also found that the number of people in insecure, low-paid work has increased by nearly one million during the Conservatives' time in office to a record 4.1 million.

There has also recently been a rise in unemployment as companies have struggled to cope in the cost-of-living crisis.

Around 4.4% of people were unemployed in the period between February and April 2024, up from the previous 4.3% figure and the highest rate since September 2021. That's about 1.5 million people.

In February this year, the UK economic inactivity rate for those aged 16 to 64 years was 22.2%, which means about 275,000 more people than a year ago.

People face debt which has built up as they have struggled to cover soaring costs. A record 6.7 million people in the UK fell behind on bills in the six months up to March 2024.

Interest rates have also led to mortgage payments rising. And as a consequence of this, landlords have increased rents. Many people face higher costs for housing.

Will energy bills come down?

Energy bills dropped in April 2024.

Ofgem's energy cap means average households will pay an average of £1,690 each year for their electricity and gas from April, the lowest level in two years.

That's down from Ofgem's price cap of £1,928 in January.

Every three months, the energy regulator reviews and updates the price cap to reflect changes in the cost of energy and inflation. It's intended to ensure bills are fair.

But it doesn't mean that your household bills can't exceed £1,690 – some households will pay more and others less. It all depends on how much energy you use, as well as your circumstances like where you live and the energy efficiency of your property.

It will to drop again to £1,568 from July, Ofgem has confirmed.

'The price cap does not protect those who simply cannot afford the cost of keeping warm,' Adam Scorer, the chief executive of National Energy Action, previously said. 'That requires direct government intervention through bill support, social tariffs and energy efficiency.'

The Government's energy rebate scheme, a discount on household energy bills, ended in March last year. This had been a lifeline to many people, helping them save around £66 each month.

Simon Francis, coordinator of the End Fuel Poverty Coalition, said: 'Three years of staggering energy bills have placed an unbearable strain on household finances up and down the country. Household energy debt is at record levels, millions of people are living in cold, damp homes and children are suffering in mouldy conditions.

'Everybody can see what is happening in Britain's broken energy system and it is time for politicians to unite to enact the measures needed to end fuel poverty. This includes cross-party consensus on a long-term plan to help all households upgrade their homes and short-term financial support for households most in need.'

Will house prices come down?

House prices are still increasing. Average UK house prices increased by 1.8% in the 12 months to March, according to official figures. The ONS said average house prices are now at £283,000.

House price increase was highest in Yorkshire and the Humber where prices increased by 2.2% in the year to March 2024. In London, however, house prices fell by 0.9%.

Meanwhile, UK private rents increased by 8.9% in the year to April. The Work Foundation has said renters in Britain are having to find £103 more a month than they were last year.

This is most acute for workers in London where rents are now 10.8% higher than in 2023, and will hit insecure workers hardest as they earn on average £3,276 less than those in secure jobs.

Rebecca Florisson, principal analyst at the Work Foundation at Lancaster University, said: 'With only 30% of employers preparing to give above inflation pay rises in 2024, many private renters will have little breathing room to pay their increased rental costs which are already outpacing wage increases.

'This will be particularly challenging for the 1.4 million private renters in severely insecure work, who are most vulnerable to rent hikes while managing irregular hours and variable pay checks.

'There is more bad news for renters as UK house prices have risen by 1.8% in the year, putting the opportunity of buying a house further out of reach for many cash-strapped private renters.'

The number of people in mortgage arrears rose 25% over 2023. Higher mortgage rates could soon hit thousands of households, with almost 900,000 UK mortgages up for renewal in the first three quarters of 2024.

But the latest boost in house prices is good news for some in the property sector. Nathan Emerson, the chief executive of Propertymark, which represents estate agents, said: 'The housing market is a key indicator regarding wider economic health, and it is extremely positive to see further uplift and confidence within the housing sector.

'As inflation tracks downwards, it is widely anticipated the Bank of England will consider a reduction in its base rate and at this point we hope to see lenders offering a much wider range of competitive and highly targeted deals.'

Are prices rising at the same rate for everyone?

Unfortunately not. Prices are rising even faster for poorer households. This is because the costs of essentials like food were soaring at high rates, and low-income families typically spend a greater proportion of their income on these items.

The Resolution Foundation has found that poorer families are most affected by surging food prices as they spend a far greater share of their family budgets on food (14%, compared to 9% for the highest-income households).

As a result, the effective inflation rate for the poorest tenth of households is around 2% higher than it is for the richest tenth of households.

Benefits are not stretching far enough to help those on the lowest incomes afford the basic essentials.

The Joseph Rowntree Foundation posted on X: 'The rate of inflation is coming down. But the damage of the last few years remains an open wound that continues to go mostly untreated.

'The prime minister says the plan is working and the chancellor says the economy is returning to full health. However, inflation is not a measure of poverty and celebrating this figure ignores the gravity of the broader context of poverty in the UK.'

The world's five richest men have £688 billion of wealth between them. That's boomed by £367 billon in the last five years.

Meanwhile, the wealth of the poorest 60% – encompassing nearly five billion people – has fallen. What does this all mean exactly? The rich are getting richer, and the poor are getting poorer.

25 June 2024

The above information is reprinted with kind permission from *The Big Issue*.
© The Big Issue Limited 2024

www.bigissue.com

Chapter 3: Poverty in the UK

Types of poverty in the UK

In the UK, an estimated 14.5 million people are living in poverty. Poverty can affect people in many different ways, some people may experience some or all of the below:

Child Poverty: Child poverty is a situation where children live in households with income levels so low that they struggle to meet their basic needs such as food, clothing, and shelter. It's more than just not having enough money; it often means missing out on opportunities that other kids have, like going on school trips or joining sports teams. Living in poverty can affect children's health, education, and overall chances in life, as they may face challenges that hinder their ability to succeed and lead a happy, fulfilling life.

Food Poverty: Food poverty is when individuals or families can't afford or access enough nutritious food, which is essential for good health and wellbeing. It means that people may go hungry, rely on unhealthy fast food because it's cheaper, or have to choose between buying food and paying other important bills. This can lead to health problems like obesity, diabetes, or heart disease, and also affects people's mood and energy, making daily life much harder.

Fuel Poverty: Being in fuel poverty means having a tough time heating or powering your home because it's too costly. Imagine during winter, not having enough money to turn the heating on, so you're cold all the time, or perhaps not being able to use the stove to cook meals. It's a big issue for people with low incomes, especially when energy prices go up. This can lead to living in cold, damp conditions which might make people sick, and it's really stressful for families trying to keep their homes warm and comfortable.

Digital Poverty: Digital poverty means not having regular access to devices like computers or smartphones and not having a decent internet connection. In today's world, that's like being locked out of a huge part of life. Many homework assignments, job applications, and government services are online, so without the digital tools, people miss out on education, job opportunities, and support. It can also make someone feel isolated, because so much socialising happens online through chats, games, and social media.

Hygiene Poverty: Hygiene poverty is when people can't afford basic hygiene products like soap, toothpaste, deodorant, and menstrual products. Imagine not being able to take a shower because there's no soap or feeling embarrassed because you can't buy deodorant. It goes beyond just feeling clean; it's about dignity and health too. When people can't access these essentials, it can affect their self-esteem, social life, and opportunities. This kind of poverty isn't always talked about, but it's a real issue that impacts people's lives, making it challenging to participate fully in school or work. By understanding hygiene poverty, we can better support and advocate for those in need, ensuring everyone has access to the basic products required to stay healthy and feel good about themselves.

Period Poverty: Period poverty refers to the struggle many girls and women face when they can't afford menstrual products like tampons or pads. This leads to missing out on normal life stuff, like going to school or work, when they have their period. It's a big deal because it can cause embarrassment, and it's unfair that having a period – which is totally natural – could stop someone from doing everyday activities. There's a growing movement to provide free menstrual products to tackle this problem.

There are many charities and programmes run to help support people who are experiencing any type of poverty, such as food-banks which not only provide food, but also toiletries and hygiene products. They also usually provide guidance and can refer you to other support services such as debt advice.

The problem is poverty, however we label it

The prefixes 'food', 'child' or 'fuel' make life for 14 million poor Britons seem easily fixable. In truth, radical action is needed.

By Aditya Chakrabortty

How ingenious are the British! Like the legendary Inuit people who coined 57 words for snow, we have devised a long list of clever aliases for the stuff that dominates everyday life. Know the ones I mean? Try food poverty. Fuel poverty. Child poverty. Clothing poverty. Transport poverty. Period poverty.

These are phrases mouthed in Westminster and plastered across newspapers (which, this week, are discussing 'digital poverty'). They help shape the UK in the 21st century. But this ever-growing jungle of subcategories obscures the one true problem they have in common. It is poverty: the condition of not having enough money to live your life.

If your only choice of an evening is between skipping dinner or going to sleep in the cold before waking up in the cold, then you are not carefully selecting between food poverty and fuel poverty, like some expense-account diner havering over the French reds on a wine list. You are simply impoverished.

If you are using a sock as a sanitary towel, the problem lies not in the time of the month but in your lack of income – which doubtless means you're also not getting enough food or heating. Gas bills might jump or petrol prices soar, but if those things tip you into all-out crisis, that's because you were already poor.

Poverty cannot be shelved tidily under different classifications, like books in a library. It jabs its tentacles into all parts of your life, distorting and defining everything from how you feel about yourself to whether you live or die in this pandemic.

'Want' was how William Beveridge referred to poverty in his landmark report of 1942. For him it was the first of five 'giant evils' that had to be slain in order to rebuild a bombed-out Britain. Today, however, it is the evil that dare not speak its name. It must instead be broken down into discrete categories, all the better to tuck into Whitehall documents or charity campaign strategies. In that fake neatness lies both great political hypocrisy and huge social danger.

Cabinet ministers hate using words as simple and shaming as poverty. It's why the welfare secretary, Thérèse Coffey, brightly refers to those forced to live on donated tins as food bank 'customers'. No, far more congenial to qualify and to narrow. Oh, it's about 'cashflow problems', as the foreign secretary, Dominic Raab, so delightfully put it. Or schoolkids not having an internet dongle.

Smaller messes take less time and money to tidy away. Whereas, according to horrified allies of Rishi Sunak this week, keeping an extra £20 on Universal Credit amid a historic jobs crisis would cost £6 billion a year, or 1p on income tax and 5p on fuel duty. Remember, in his first budget speech last March, Sunak admitted that Tory chancellors freezing fuel duty for nine years had cost the exchequer £110 billion – and then froze it for another year.

Because anything is better than admitting that this all stems from one deep structural problem: that, going into the pandemic, more than 14 million Britons – more than one in five of us – did not have enough money to live on. Far more agreeable to dole out food parcels for a week here or there, to cut VAT on tampons, or to brief a couple of warning headlines aimed at the big energy firms.

Much better to wave around vouchers and an outsourced half-pepper than give money and power to people who have none. Because who knows what the poor might do if they were to – whisper it – choose for themselves? This is why Coffey's predecessor, Iain Duncan Smith, blamed the problem of child poverty not on his colleagues slashing benefits – so as to teach mums and dads that 'children cost money' – but on the parents themselves being drunks and smack addicts.

In IDS's world, the undeserving poor are always with us. The undeserving rich, such as he, on the other hand, get to marry the daughter of a baron, live in a £2 million mansion owned by an obliging father-in-law, and deliver speeches to moneymen at £5,000 a time.

Such are the deep prejudices faced by campaigners down the ages. The Child Poverty Action Group was formed 56 years ago, but at the outset its activists had no special interest in child poverty. The charity's official history states: '"Child poverty" was not mentioned in the minutes of meetings. As the committee members saw it, poor children lived in poor families.' But just weeks before launch: '"Child Poverty Action Group" was adopted as the name … as likely to win more public sympathy than "family poverty", which risked inciting rightwing tabloid rants about "scroungers"'.

This was in 1965, several years before George Osborne was even conceived. What giant strides this country has made.

Even so, those founders were spot on. In my years of reporting on poverty and inequality, one reliable rule of thumb is that the kids are last to go without. First to starve are the mums. They're the ones who live on hot water and toast to keep the family in meals. But the terminally prejudiced cannot bear too much reality, and it is they who set the tone of the debate.

In his recent book *The New Poverty*, the journalist Stephen Armstrong recounts how the Archbishop of Canterbury, Justin Welby, travelled in 2015 to Folkestone in Kent, where he met Graham and Lisa Sopp. The couple had moved there after Graham had lost his job as a security guard and Lisa was promised cleaning work. Then their new flat fell through, Lisa's employer was taken over, and one of IDS's benefits offices kept messing them about. Suddenly, they were sleeping in a tent on the cliffs, and Graham got very ill. They took to walking the clifftops, identifying the perfect spot from which to jump.

On meeting them, Welby observed: 'There is no system in the world that will stop people having problems, but we must have a structure of support for people that meets not merely their financial needs but also their need to be treated as distinct human beings of infinite value.' That view doesn't fit with a system where poor people queue for bags of surplus food, collect donated clothes for their babies and beg for help with their fuel bills and housing.

The new language of poverty, so managerial and sophisticated, conceals a vast and growing baseness. However highly evolved its jargon, however lauded its campaigning footballers, Britain in 2021 treats poor people not as people – not as our family, friends, neighbours. Instead, it views them as a ragbag of different physical needs to be met by a patchwork of largely volunteer organisations. And in doing so, we deny both their essential humanity – and ours.

21 January 2021

Consider!

This article was written in 2021 – how do you think things have changed since then?

Questions

? What were the five 'giant evils' mentioned in the *Beveridge Report*? (You may have to do some independent research for this.)

? When was the *Beveridge Report* published?

? Who was William Beveridge?

Debate

'Poverty cannot be shelved tidily under different classifications, like books in a library.'

As a class, debate the statement above. Do you agree or disagree?

The above information is reprinted with kind permission from *The Guardian*.
© 2024 Guardian News and Media Limited

www.theguardian.com

What is food poverty?

Food poverty encompasses both the affordability of food and its accessibility within local communities. There is no agreed definition but here are three interpretations that Sustain believes set out the scope of the problem:

'The inability to afford, or to have access to, food to make up a healthy diet.' – The Department of Health

'Food poverty is worse diet, worse access, worse health, higher percentage of income on food and less choice from a restricted range of foods.' – Professor Tim Lang

'The inability to consume an adequate quality or sufficient quantity of food in socially acceptable ways, or the uncertainty that one will be able to do so.' – Professor Elizabeth Dowler

Other terms to describe food poverty include household food insecurity, food insecurity, food vulnerability and hunger.

Causes and impact

Food poverty can be triggered by a crisis in finances or personal circumstances. This could include job losses, changes in housing, a delay in receiving Universal Credit, an unexpected expense, or family bereavement. It can also be a long-term experience of not being able to access or have the facilities to prepare a healthy diet. For example, low wages that do not cover the cost-of-living or a disability that prevents an individual from accessing healthy food as needed.

Once these circumstances have been triggered, food budgets are often the first thing to be cut to accommodate for other vital living costs such as rent and fuel.

Food poverty has multiple negative impacts on individuals' health and wellbeing, including a higher risk of dietary related illnesses and diseases due to healthy and nutritious food often being more expensive than food high in fat, salt and sugar.

Who is most at risk?

To understand who is at risk we must first know how many people are living in food poverty. 5 million people in the UK lived in food poverty between 2019 and 2020, according to the Governments latest Family Resources Survey. In 2020, this was 8% of the population, but data from The Food Foundation suggests food insecurity levels rose to 9% of the population in January 2021. The Trussell Trust has also seen an increase in food bank use of 123% over the past five years, whilst the Independent Food Aid Network report a rise of 110% between 2019 and 2020.

It's safe to say that food poverty in the UK is rising, whether it be 8 or 9% of the population, and anyone can be affected. Children who are unable to access free school meals during the holidays; individuals who are using food banks for the first time after a job loss; parents on low incomes who skip meals so their children can eat; older people unable to prepare meals without support, or people with no recourse to public funds who are excluded from most welfare support.

All of these instances are a symptom of inadequate and/or insecure incomes, holes in the welfare safety net, increased living costs, rising debt, and financial problems for households living with disability and mental health issues.

These symptoms don't affect people equally though. The Governments own figures state that household food insecurity rises from 8% of the population to 19% for Black led households and 41% for households with three or more children. In 2020 analysis found that two in three households referred to a Trussell Trust food bank included one or more disabled people. The Covid-19 outbreak has only exacerbated this disproportionate impact. For example, Bangladeshi (43%) and Black British groups (38%) were most likely to report a loss of income since Covid-19, leaving them vulnerable to household food insecurity.

The need for action

Sustain believes that modern-day hunger is unacceptable, and we are working to end it through projects and campaigns that change policy and practice at the national and local level. Many councils, community groups and others are taking action to ensure people are able to eat and to address the root causes of people's difficulties.

However, major cuts to local authority budgets, the welfare safety net, and rising fuel, food and housing costs undermine these local efforts. To change this, we need to support local coordination and push government, councils and other statutory organisations to take responsibility for ending hunger. This would ensure local communities are able to access healthy, affordable food in a dignified manner and push governments to rebalance the burden of responsibility that currently falls far too heavily on local actors.

Design

Design a poster with details of your local food bank, and to encourage donations to the food bank. Some food banks have lists of needed food items, try to include this on your poster.

The above information is reprinted with kind permission from Sustain.

© Sustain 2024

www.sustainweb.org

Food banks in the UK

The Trussell Trust, an anti-poverty charity that operates a network of food banks across the UK, reported a 37% increase in the number of three-day emergency food parcels it distributed between 31 March 2022 and 1 April 2023, compared to the year before.

By Brigid Francis-Devine

The Trussell Trust, an anti-poverty charity that operates a network of food banks across the UK, reported a 37% increase in demand for food parcels between 2021/22 and 2022/23 and another 4% increase between 2022/23 and 2023/24. This continues a general trend of increasing need for food parcels.

How many food banks are there in the UK?

The Trussell Trust distributed parcels from 1,699 locations across the UK in 2023/24 and there are at least 1,172 additional independent food banks. The chart below shows the number of food parcels distributed by the Trussell Trust each year to 2023/24.

London was the region with the highest distribution of Trussell Trust food parcels in 2023/24, followed by the North West of England.

People using food banks

The DWP published food bank data for the first time in 2023. In its Households Below Average Income (HBAI) statistics, it reported that 3% of all individuals in the UK used a food bank in the previous 12 months in 2022/23.

In June 2023 the Trussell Trust published a report on Hunger in the UK. The report examined the causes of hunger in the UK, its impact and what type of people use food banks. Some of the headline findings of the report are:

- Disabled people make up 26% of the UK population and 69% of people referred to Trussell Trust food banks.
- People who live in social housing make up 8% of the UK population and 46% of those referred to a food bank. Renters make up 22% of the UK population and 68% of those referred to food banks.
- 89% of people referred to Trussell Trust food banks receive means tested benefits.

The rising cost-of-living means more demand for food banks

The Independent Food Aid Network surveyed its food banks in March 2024 and nearly 75% of respondents said they experienced increased demand in November 2023 to January 2024 compared to the same period a year before. 98% of them supported people seeking help for the first time.

Citizen's Advice helped 19,810 people with food bank referrals in April 2024, up from 15,675 April 2023 and 13,208 in April 2022. Food bank referrals peaked in January 2024, when Citizen's Advice helped 22,452 people.

The rising cost-of-living means a fall in food donations. In November 2023 to January 2024, 65% of IFAN organisations reported a drop in food donations and 45% reported a drop in financial donations compared with the same period a year before. The Trussell Trust also reported that some of its food banks were seeing decreased donations in 2023/24. Overall, donations of food to the Trussell Trust in 2023/24 remained at similar levels to the previous year, but since demand has increased, they had to purchase more food than ever before.

28 May 2024

The above information is reprinted with kind permission from UK Parliament.
© UK Parliament 2024
This information is licensed under the Open Parliament Licence v3.0
To view this licence, visit https://www.parliament.uk/site-information/copyright-parliament/open-parliament-licence/

www.parliament.uk

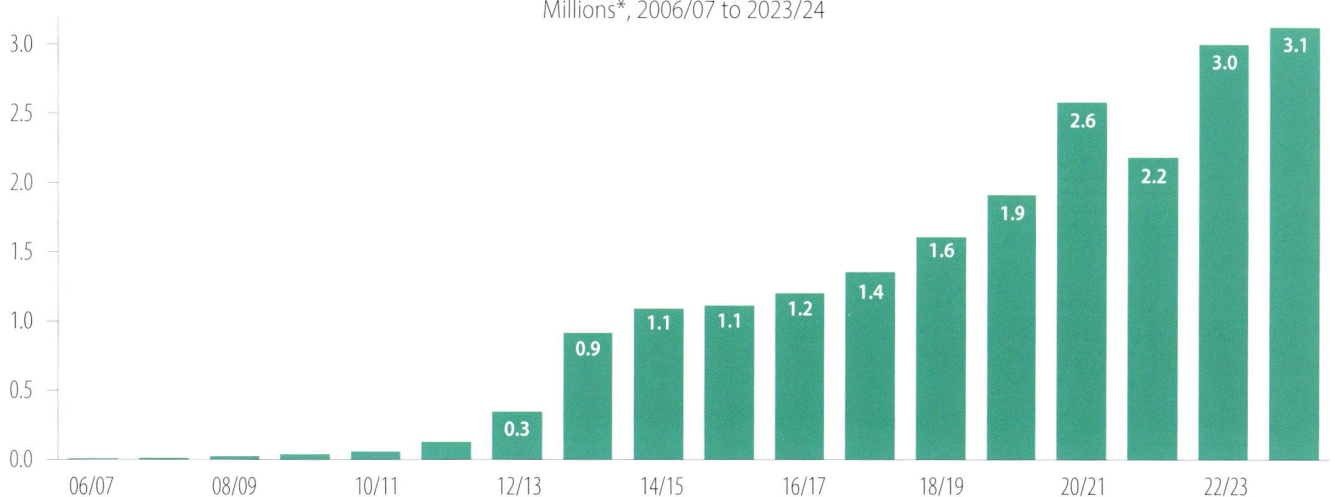

Trussell Trust emergency food supply parcels
Millions*, 2006/07 to 2023/24

*Number of parcels supplied, not the number of individuals receiving them.
Source: Trussell Trust End of Year Stats April 2023 – March 2024

'They don't have enough' – schools in England are running food banks for families

An article from *The Conversation*.

By Will Bake, Senior Lecturer, School of Education, University of Bristol

The peak of the cost-of-living crisis may have passed, but millions of families are struggling to buy enough food to feed their children. Experiencing food insecurity can be deeply damaging for children and negatively affects their achievement at school.

My research, alongside other studies, shows that schools are operating their own food banks and providing charitable food aid to families. This shows how the education system – from early years to secondary schools – is increasingly at the front line in responding to child poverty, food insecurity, and destitution.

At the start of the financial crisis in 2008 there were few food banks in the UK. Now they are in towns and cities across the country. In 2010–11, charity the Trussell Trust operated 35 food bank centres. Now, the charity runs over 1,400.

Recent research from the charity the Food Foundation estimates that one in five families with children do not have secure access to food.

After almost a decade and a half of Conservative governments, a significant number of schools are running food banks to support families and children.

I interviewed school staff at 25 schools across England, in towns and cities including Bristol, Liverpool and London. I wanted to understand how and why schools are providing charitable food to families.

The message was clear: schools were running food banks because they were faced with growing poverty and families struggling financially. Parents can't afford to buy food or pay bills, and turn to schools for help. As one staff member I spoke to said:

'They don't have enough food, they don't eat typically well because they can't afford it, and that's no fault of their own.'

Teachers talked about the cost-of-living crisis and changes to the UK's benefit system – in particular the replacement of a number of previous benefit allowances with Universal Credit – as reasons the food banks were necessary. Research has suggested that the switch to Universal Credit is leaving some families worse off. 'It's less than what they're on before. And we have that period where you swap [systems] where you haven't got any money,' one teacher said.

Some of the families supported by school food banks did not qualify for free school meals for their children but were still struggling. Commenting on who made use of the food bank, one teacher said:

'Sometimes it's the ones who have free school meals and sometimes it's the next lot up that are working families and just have absolutely no money at all and no-one to support them or help them with that because they just miss it.'

The growth of food banks in schools shows how schools are often acting as an emergency service. 'The government has dismantled public services over the past decade and schools are the last people standing,' Ann Longfield, former children's commissioner for England, has recently commented.

A growing problem

The latest research I am working on with colleagues throws the situation facing families and schools into even starker relief. We are currently investigating how many school-based food banks there are in England and the sorts of schools they are located in.

Our new research, which has not yet been published in a peer-reviewed journal, suggests that 21% of primary and secondary schools operate some kind of food bank. We estimate that this amounts to over 4,000 school-based food banks across England.

This would mean that there are now more food banks inside schools than the combined total of food banks operated by charities the Trussell Trust – the UK's largest food bank operator – and the Independent Food Aid Network.

If schools are now systematically supporting families through charitable food aid, they need guidance, support and funding. Families need well-paid and secure work and a social security system that provides people with both dignity and the financial means to buy essentials, which includes being able to buy food and clothes and heat their homes.

It's worth remembering that the goal of a well-functioning welfare state should be to prevent poverty and destitution in the first place rather than provide relief for them after the fact.

Plans to dramatically reduce child poverty, food insecurity and inequality must be central to all political parties' election manifestos.

17 April 2024

THE CONVERSATION

The above information is reprinted with kind permission from The Conversation.
© 2010-2024, The Conversation Trust (UK) Limited

www.theconversation.com

More school children to arrive in school with 'dirty clothes and unbrushed teeth' amid increase in hygiene poverty

Nearly three in four school staff believe there has been an increase in 'hygiene poverty' issues in their school in the last year.

By Eleanor Busby

More children are likely to arrive at school this term with unclean clothes and unbrushed teeth, teachers have suggested.

Nearly three in four (72%) school staff believe there has been an increase in 'hygiene poverty' issues in their school in the last year, according to a poll.

The survey, of 500 school staff in the UK who had said they were aware of pupils experiencing hygiene poverty, suggests that 71% expect the levels of hygiene poverty to have increased by the start of the school year this month.

Dirty uniforms and PE kits, unwashed hair and unclean teeth were the most cited indicators of hygiene poverty by the staff questioned in June.

The poll, carried out for charity The Hygiene Bank and cleaning brand smol, defines hygiene poverty as those who are 'caught between being able to heat their home, pay their bills, buy food or keep clean'.

Some of the school staff reported personally washing uniforms and PE kits for children at home, and handing out laundry detergent for families in need.

The survey, which was conducted by market research platform Attest, suggests that 72% of school staff said they had seen pupils affected by hygiene poverty experience low self-esteem.

Meanwhile, 53% of school staff said these pupils were isolated or 'left out' by other pupils in class, and 50% said they had seen a negative impact on mental health for those experiencing hygiene poverty.

More than a quarter (26%) of school staff said they had seen absenteeism as a result of hygiene poverty.

One respondent said: 'Students are often left with no desk partner in class. Makes it awkward for staff members to deal with the situation. Students are often faced with working alone. Other students make nasty comments in front of the class to single them out.'

Another respondent said they had 'a feeling of powerlessness' that they could not do more.

'Many schools routinely help out by discreetly washing clothes and providing items of uniform'. — Julie McCulloch, ASCL

Sarah Smith, executive headteacher of St Cuthbert's Catholic Academy, a primary school in Blackpool, said: 'We have seen an increase in students coming to school with unwashed uniforms and we know that this has an effect on their mental health and overall wellbeing, which in turn will have a negative impact on their education.'

Brand smol, in collaboration with The Hygiene Bank, is hoping to expand its Suds in Schools initiative, which provides mini laundrettes to schools, so more families in need are provided with clean clothes.

Suds in Schools wants to raise £25,000 to establish an additional 25 laundrettes in UK schools.

Lucy Wishart, of smol, said: 'With hygiene poverty increasing, it's more important than ever for us to support more schools.'

She added: 'We believe that everyone should have access to clean clothes, in order to live their life to the fullest, and our research shows just how much this can impact young people at a crucial stage in their academic and social lives.'

Julie McCulloch, director of policy at the Association of School and College Leaders (ASCL), said: 'Hygiene poverty is linked to very high levels of deprivation as families struggle with the cost of things like washing machines, energy bills and clothes.

'Many schools routinely help out by discreetly washing clothes and providing items of uniform.

'This has long been the case but has become more of an issue following the pandemic and cost-of-living crisis as more families struggle financially.

'The level of child poverty in the UK is utterly unacceptable and the government must do more to tackle the problem.'

4 September 2023

The above information is reprinted with kind permission from *The Independent*.
© independent.co.uk 2024

www.independent.co.uk

Wet wipe showers and washing up liquid for shampoo: How it feels to live in hygiene poverty

By Sarah Ingram

Last September, Chantel Graham made an appointment with her doctor.

Although only 38, she couldn't understand why her memory had apparently stopped working; she would forget things, get confused and was scared that she had dementia.

The single mum-of-two from London remembers: 'It was little things. I was locking myself out of my bank, forgetting passwords, or they would ask me 'what's your memorable word' – and I didn't have a clue at all.

'I was so tired. My brain would just wipe. I would completely forget to see people I'd arranged to meet up with. I would forget whole conversations.'

After going through tests, it emerged that Chantel didn't have a terrifying brain disease – the problem was, in fact, stress. The anxiety of struggling to pay the bills and feeding her kids had messed with her memory.

Chantel had been living in 'survival mode' since 2020 when Covid-19 forced her to go on unpaid leave from her job as cabin crew. She claimed benefits and scrimped and saved, but the benefits only covered her rent, and she ended up in food and hygiene poverty, broken and exhausted.

'Hygiene poverty' is the term used to describe the inability to afford everyday cleaning and personal grooming products that many of us take for granted. A shocking nine million UK adults (one in six) now live in hygiene poverty – a figure that has tripled over the last year – according to research last month from charity In Kind Direct, an organisation that provides consumer products (donated by household manufacturers, retailers and brands) to charities.

Food bank users report using wet wipes instead of hot showers, or using washing up liquid as body wash and shampoo. Up and down the UK, families like Chantel's have been forced to choose between groceries and grooming.

'I'd been playing the strong, Black mum, but my body told me; we can't cope with this,' she explains. 'It was the stress and the worry of how I would get through it when the bills kept coming. I've never experienced that level of uncertainty.'

Chantel tried not to concern her two daughters, now age five and nine, while cutting back on every possible purchase; replacing shower gels and bubble bath with soap and bicarbonate of soda, hand washing their school clothes with washing up liquid in the sink, and cutting open the tubes to eek out every last scraping of toothpaste.

She remembers: 'I played it down to the kids, but I was feeling like a complete failure as a mum. Those little things all add up; the shampoo, the loo roll, sanitary products. They've all gone up so much in price and it gets unmanageable. Things that I never thought about before, that I used to just pick up and put in the trolley, I couldn't afford. It was a horrible time. I didn't know what to do or who to turn to for help.

'I felt like a failure; that I'd let my kids down,' adds Chantel. 'I'd been down every avenue for help that I could think of and they were all closed. Things got really hard for me. I couldn't work, I couldn't not work. I just didn't know what to do.

'I was having trouble sleeping, I lost weight and I had brain fog. I was doing my best to look after the kids, but I was just on autopilot. I really struggled.'

One of the hardest parts was buying period products. Chantel has sensitive skin, and some brands bring her out in rashes. But she had to revert to the thickest, cheapest available sanitary towels, an unpleasant experience that reminded her of having just given birth.

'It was so stressful More school children to arrive in school with 'dirty clothes and unbrushed teeth' amid increase in hygiene poverty – and the shock of it, to go from travelling around the world to going to the supermarket and not being able to afford things,' she says. 'Sanitary products are so expensive and the overnight pads I bought – they weren't nice. It affects your self-esteem and I felt self-conscious buying them.'

It's a problem facing women all over the country. One told In Kind Direct: 'Having to choose between period products and washing products can be the difference in a full food shop and having to choose what to put back. This shouldn't be a choice for anyone.'

While another has said: 'My mum doesn't always have enough money to buy period products. There are three of us in the house and we all need them. The cheaper ones leak and then we have to do more laundry. Then having to dry the clothes inside in winter adds further cost. We don't know what to do.'

Three in five people who live in hygiene poverty suffer from poor mental health as a result, according to Ruth Brock, CEO of The Hygiene Bank, a community-led charity that provides people with products, and was the chosen charity for Metro.co.uk's 2020 Lifeline campaign.

The Hygiene Bank has seen consistently higher demand in recent months, with waiting lists having doubled throughout the cost-of-living crisis.

'Hygiene poverty makes people isolate themselves from friends, family and even opportunities at school and work. It is uniquely oppressive,' Ruth explains. 'Our research and work in local communities show the impact of hygiene poverty on people's self-esteem. From teenagers skipping school, and people isolating themselves in their homes, to parents who don't even feel comfortable joining a nursery collection queue because of the shame and embarrassment they feel about their appearance.'

Lesley Crellin relies on a food bank to get by, and when she brings a new bottle of washing up liquid home, she pours half into an empty bottle and tops them both up with water. She's been struggling with the bills since the cost-of-living crisis hit, and has been unable to work since she had a stroke 20 years ago. Lesley manages other health issues and is a carer for her husband Tony, who is terminally ill, meaning the couple rely on benefits.

For Lesley, 59 from Crewe, hygiene and cleaning products were the first to go when things got tight. She makes savings wherever she can; she's cleaned clothes with washing up liquid, uses the bare minimum detergent in the washing machine – which she barely runs – only showers every other day and she's abandoned hope of buying household basics like glass cleaner or air freshener.

She tells Metro.co.uk: 'It's a constant struggle. You get stuck as to whether you buy food or pay your bills. It's been really hard. Even toothpaste is expensive now. I very rarely buy anything to do with hygiene or washing from the supermarket.

'I find it difficult and it gets me down. It's hard when I get to the supermarket; I don't go up the cleaning aisles, the products aisle, I don't go up the cereal aisle. I can't afford it.'

For the past four years, Lesley has been visiting Chance, a charity that supports the homeless and vulnerable in Crewe and Nantwich, every Monday, where for £3.50 she can get a good amount of food, toilet roll, washing powder and hygiene and sanitary products and other goods.

'I was cutting down wherever I could; watering down the shampoo and shower gel and washing less,' she adds. 'I had to cut down drastically on everything. I used to like having two showers a day, and washing my hair every day, but I was only having two or three showers a week. It's terrible when you can't have a shower when you want to. You don't feel fresh. You feel untidy. It made me feel like I wasn't looking after myself.

'If it wasn't for Chance I wouldn't have any of this stuff. I certainly wouldn't be buying deodorant and toothpaste. I can't afford £6 or £7 for washing powder. I would just go without and I would find it so hard. I'm so very grateful to them.'

Lesley's struggle is compounded by her husband's diagnosis of interstitial lung disease, emphysema and COPD in April last year which has left him on a transplant list.

'I'm so worried. I sit here, day after day and I think – how am I going to have a funeral? I've got no money,' she admits. 'When the inevitable comes, which I know it will, how am I going to bury him?

'It's 2023; these are basic things that people should be able to afford to buy. Everybody should be able to afford to buy a bar of soap, some deodorant and shampoo and have a wash. It's tragic when you look at families that are struggling.'

Access to basic hygiene products are essential to maintain good mental and physical health, according to Hayley Smith, founder of FlowAid, which campaigns for free sanitary products for homeless women.

How you can help

Paul Buchanan, Interim CEO of In Kind Direct, says: 'The cost-of-living crisis has had an incredibly detrimental effect on so many low-income families across the UK, forcing them to make impossible choices between eating, heating their home and keeping clean. Everyone deserves to wake up and feel clean. Donating £10 could help supply 6 hygiene packs, reducing the pressure on 6 families for a month.

Natalie Gourlay, Head of Environmental Social Governance at Boots adds: 'In Boots stores across the country, we have over 700 donation points which offer accessible drop off points where anyone can donate essential hygiene products, bought from any shop. Our store teams work with The Hygiene Bank's network of local volunteers to distribute these items to schools, charities, local authority services and voluntary organisations, to ultimately reach those who are in need within their communities.'

'There is a shame and stigma attached to hygiene poverty and this embarrassment and fear of being judged can stop people asking for help, meaning that they get stuck in a vicious cycle,' she says. 'This can lead to further mental health issues. Physical health issues are also a worrying concern when it comes to hygiene poverty. Women who suffer are at higher risk of infection, and toxic shock syndrome is also prominent amongst homeless and vulnerable women due to prolonged use of tampons. Severe cases of TSS can lead to amputations and can also be fatal.

'Lack of poor hygiene and access to products can also cause body odour, rashes, itchiness and other diseases, which again can lead to poor mental health and feed into the stigma of embarrassment. It really can be a never ending cycle.'

Happily, Chantel is now back at work and being paid again. Like Lesley, she relied on a food bank – the Breadline in London – to get by. She is now repaying the money she borrowed on credit cards through a difficult three years, and is looking on the bright side.

'It was a really difficult time, but it is important that people know that there is support out there,' she says. 'And it was important for my daughters to see that mum needed help and that sometimes you have to ask for it. I want people to know that they're not alone.

'I'm so grateful for Breadline and InKind Direct's help. I could have cried the first time I saw that food parcel full of food and products – it was such a blessing. We'd been living off beige food – but there were fruit and vegetables! I felt like I could breathe again for the first time in a long time.'

21 May 2023

The above information is reprinted with kind permission from *Metro* & DMG Media Licensing.
© 2024 Associated Newspapers Ltd

www.metro.co.uk

Cost-of-living: UK period poverty has risen from 12% to 21% in a year

An ActionAid poll has found that the number of UK women and people who menstruate who are struggling to afford period products has risen from 12% to 21% in one year.

By Hollie Pycroft

As the cost-of-living continues to bite, a new ActionAid poll has revealed that 21% (more than one in five) women and people who menstruate in the UK are now struggling to afford period products - up from 12% in just one year. This amounts to an estimated 2.8 million people, putting around one million more people into period poverty versus last year.

Of those affected by period poverty, 41% kept sanitary pads or tampons in for longer, and 8% re-used disposable pads, which can be a dangerous method of period management.

37% said they had used tissues or cotton wool instead of sanitary products in the last 12 months. 13% used socks or other clothing, and 9% resorted to using paper or newspaper.

More than a quarter of survey respondents (28%) said they were able to rely on period products available at school or work, but for 17% they stayed at home. This means missing out on school, work, exercising or socialising, all of which can have wider implications for their mental health, wellbeing, and future.

Prioritising other essentials over period products

As the cost of everyday items continues to soar, women and people who menstruate are being forced to make difficult decisions about which essentials they can buy.

Those affected by period poverty said they were prioritising other everyday basics over the period products they need:

- 60% had to prioritise food.
- 48% had to prioritise gas/electricity.
- 24% sacrificed period products for themselves so they could afford period products for their dependant.

Those aged 18–24 were most likely to struggle to afford period products: more than a quarter (27%) of people surveyed in this age group said they were affected.

Periods forcing women to stay home

Due to period poverty, but also because of issues like the ongoing stigma around periods, our survey reveals that missing school, work, avoiding exercise or socialising are all too common for those who menstruate.

A shocking 14% of survey respondents said they have avoided or missed work during their period, while 13% have missed school or university or college.

39% missed sport or exercise, while 25% missed socialising with friends while on their periods. For 18– to 24-year-old women and people who menstruate, this amounted to 48% – almost half.

Of those who avoided or missed some activities as a result of being on their period, 32% did so because they didn't feel comfortable wearing the uniform, kit or clothing required for doing the activity. 7% missed activities because they feared being bullied or teased. 64% missed these activities because of period side effects including fatigue and anxiety.

More young women and people who menstruate feel embarrassed during their period

Despite efforts in recent years to improve openness about periods, and reduce the societal stigma (take, for example, the England Lionesses' switch to blue shorts after players voiced period concerns), it has emerged that 'period positivity' may be in decline.

Our survey found that 22% of young women and people who menstruate (aged 18–24) in the UK today feel embarrassed during their period – a significant rise from 8% in 2022.

Of those who reported feelings of anxiety, embarrassment or shame, 12% said this was because of jokes made about their period by a partner, friends, colleagues or parents. 30% said it was because people would see them taking sanitary products to the toilet, and 58% said it was because of fear of leaking onto their clothes.

This much is sadly clear: not only do significant numbers of women, girls and people who menstruate frequently feel negatively about their periods, but progress is not being made.

In the UK, as in every country around the world, people who menstruate are routinely mocked for this natural process and/or made to feel shame.

Many of us know what it's like to lend a tampon or a pad to someone – anyone – who needs one. It doesn't matter if it's your sister, a friend, or a complete stranger in the loo. It's an unwritten rule that we always help out in an emergency, if we can.

27 May 2022

The above information is reprinted with kind permission from ActionAid.
© 2024 ActionAid

www.actionaid.org.uk

How is the cost-of-living crisis affecting period poverty in the UK?

Rising prices are increasing the cost of period products, both for individuals and the charities that support those experiencing period poverty. Demand for free or affordable tampons and pads, as well as the use of hygiene banks, is growing, as budgets are squeezed.

By Gemma Williams

The cost-of-living crisis is contributing to an increase in demand for free and affordable period products. The lack of access to tampons and pads due to financial constraints – known as 'period poverty' – is on the rise in the UK. In the first three months of 2022, the charity Bloody Good Period reported a 78% increase in the need for free period products.

Period poverty is often talked about in terms of financial hardship, where people struggle to afford period products. In 2019, the UK government pledged to end period poverty by 2030. Their approach has varied greatly across the country, with policies to improve access to products being introduced in some, but not all, areas.

These include the Welsh government's provision of £1 million to tackle period poverty, the Department for Education's 'Period Products Scheme' in England, the passing of Scotland's 'Period Products (Free Provision) Bill' and the approval of a pilot project to provide period products in all primary and secondary schools in Northern Ireland.

In addition, the 'tampon tax' was abolished in January 2021, scrapping the 5% VAT on disposable period products nationwide, in recognition that period products are essential items.

Why is period poverty still such a problem?

Research shows that many people struggled to access period products during the pandemic and continue to do so today. In a study surveying 240 people, 85% stated they had difficulties getting period products during lockdown. Of these, 30% reported that this was due to financial problems, including losing their jobs or being furloughed (Williams et al., 2022).

Non-profit organisations that provide access to free period products experienced huge increases in demand for products during the pandemic, highlighting some of the reasons why period poverty increased despite the introduction of government policies to address the issue.

The reasons for this rise included the emergence of new groups experiencing period poverty for the first time (such as students and NHS staff), supply shortages and hoarding of products, the closure of places that would normally provide access to products (such as schools, libraries and public toilets) and the failure to recognise period products as 'essential items' in care packages for those who were shielding.

Although lockdown measures were lifted in the UK in July 2021, concerns over funding uncertainties and central support remain for the organisations that provide support to those experiencing period poverty. Much of this is linked to the shift in government priorities during the pandemic.

Non-profit organisations will continue to provide the majority of support, until the policies introduced to improve access to free period products are effectively implemented across the whole of the UK.

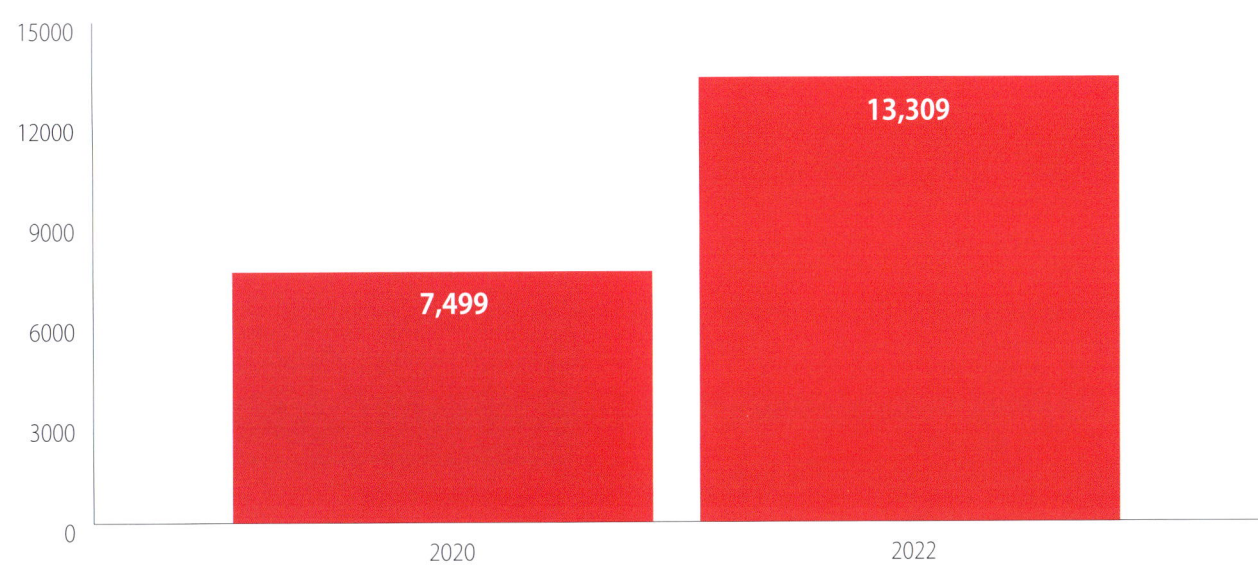

Number of free packs distributed — by year

2020: 7,499
2022: 13,309

Source: Bloody Good Period

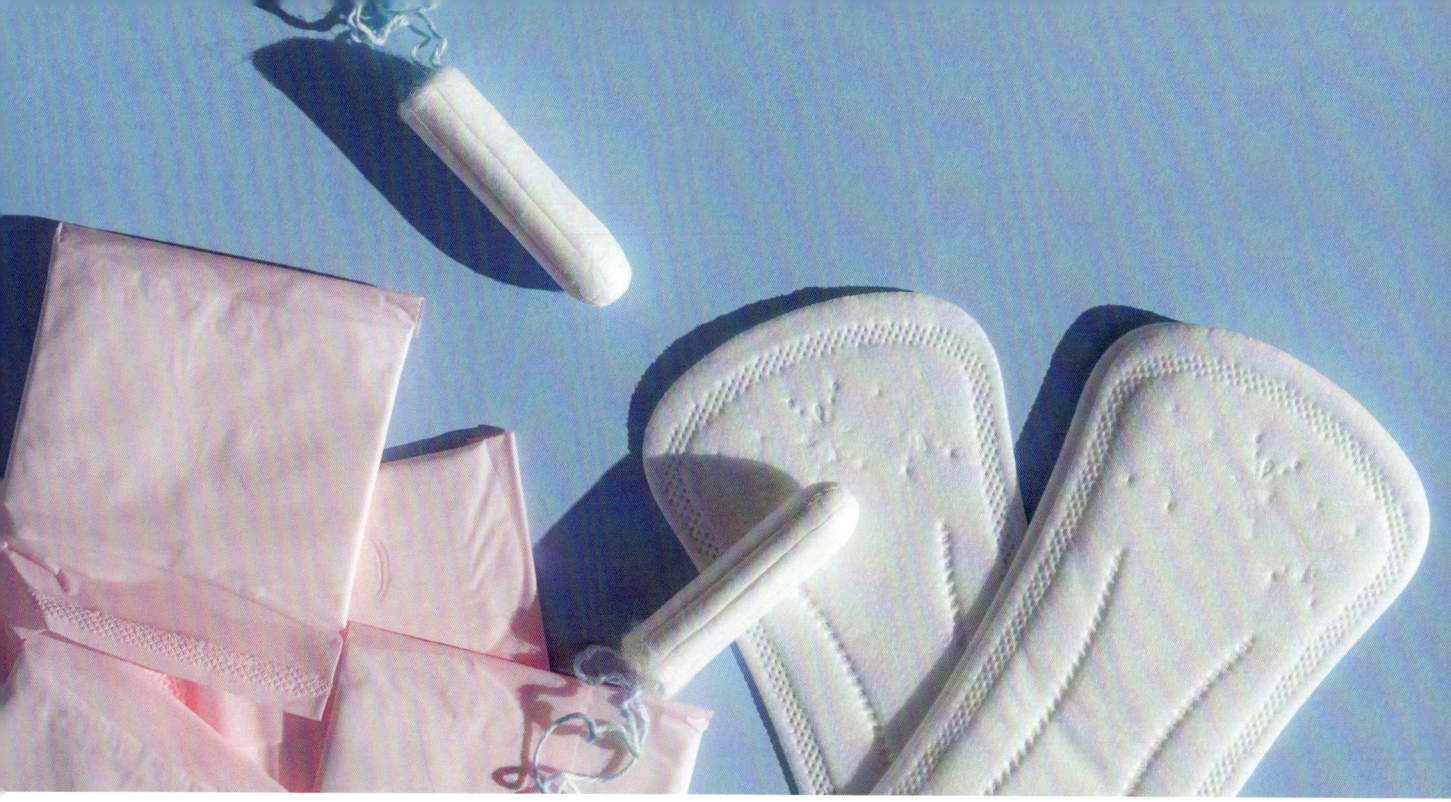

What about the cost-of-living crisis?

There is a risk that rising prices will further exacerbate period poverty in the UK. There have already been reports of large increases in demand for products as a result of the cost-of-living crisis during the first quarter of 2022.

People are having to choose between essentials as the cost of energy and food continues to rise. In this case, hygiene essentials – which include period products – are often forsaken. As a result, there has been a rise in the use of 'hygiene banks' – services that provide access to toiletries and other essential hygiene items including soap, toothpaste, cleaning products and nappies (as well as period products).

An increase in the production cost of disposable period products due to inflation and supply issues is also having an effect. Some supermarkets and suppliers have increased the cost of such period products. Tesco, for example, has doubled the price of its least expensive period pads from two pence per pad (23p for a pack) to four pence per pad (42p for a pack). This means that any gains made with the abolition of the 5% VAT tampon tax have been wiped out.

The rising costs of period products will not only affect the ability of women, girls and people who menstruate to buy these essential items but will also mean that non-profit organisations will find it increasingly difficult to purchase the quantity of products they need to meet increasing demand.

This increase, coupled with a decrease in donations that such organisations would typically receive as people reprioritise their spending, could further hinder their ability to continue to provide support for those experiencing period poverty.

What are the implications of rising period poverty?

There is currently no consistent central government strategy or funding in place to address period poverty, despite claims that money would be available. In 2019, the then Minister for Women and Equalities, Penny Mordaunt, stated that the government would provide '£2 million funding through UK Aid Direct to projects to help women and girls living in poverty to manage their periods with dignity'. Also promised was a further £250,000 of seed funding from the Government Equalities Office 'to support the work of the [period poverty] taskforce'. It is still not known how or if this money has been spent.

With the pandemic and the cost-of-living crisis making the situation worse for people experiencing period poverty, as well as for organisations providing support for these individuals, there is a clear need for the UK government to honour its pledge to 'end period poverty by 2030'. Until then, the cost-of-living crisis is likely to have a disproportionate effect on women, girls and people who menstruate from lower-income households.

4 July 2022

Activity

In small groups, find out the average yearly cost for period products. Compare both the lowest and highest costs. Do any products work out more cost-effective? Are disposable or reusable products cheaper?

Key facts

- In the first three months of 2022, the charity Bloody Good Period reported a 78% increase in the need for free period products.

- The 'tampon tax' was abolished in January 2021, scrapping the 5% VAT on disposable period products.

The above information is reprinted with kind permission from Economics Observatory.

© 2024 Economics Observatory

www.economicsobservatory.com

Where can I find help?

Below are some telephone numbers, email addresses and websites of agencies or charities that can offer support or advice if you, or someone you know, needs it.

Debt advice

If you need advice on any of your debts/concerns about money, please seek free advice from a charity. There are many companies that charge for the debt solutions, but free help is available.

Citizen's Advice
www.citizensadvice.org.uk

Christians Against Poverty
www.capuk.org

Debt Advice Foundation
Tel: 0800 043 40 50 (Monday to Friday, 8am to 6pm)
www.debtadvicefoundation.org

entitledto
Free benefits calculator to help you find out what you are entitled to.
www.entitledto.co.uk

MoneyHelper
www.moneyhelper.org.uk

Money Saving Expert
www.moneysavingexpert.com

National Debtline
Helpline: 0808 808 4000 (9am-8pm)
www.nationaldebtline.org

Salvation Army
www.salvationarmy.org.uk

StepChange Debt Charity
Helpline: 0800 138 1111
www.stepchange.org

Turn2us
Helpline: 0808 802 2000
www.turn2us.org.uk

Food Banks

If you are in need of help with food, you will need a referral to a food bank. You can ask your nearest Citizens Advice to refer you to a food bank, or your GP, housing association or social worker. Your local council may also be able to tell you how to get a referral.

Citizen's Advice
www.citizensadvice.org.uk

Salvation Army food banks
www.salvationarmy.org.uk/foodbanks

Trussell Trust
Helpline: 0808 208 2138
www.trussell.org.uk

Money Saving Apps

These apps are a great way to get free, or reduced cost food.

Olio
www.olioapp.com

Too Good To Go
toogoodtogo.com

Useful Websites

Useful websites

www.actionaid.org.uk

www.bigissue.com

www.economicsobservatory.com

www.independent.co.uk

www.investigate-europe.eu

www.jrf.org.uk

www.metro.co.uk

www.parliament.uk

www.prospectmagazine.co.uk

www.rescue.org

www.sustainweb.org

www.theconversation.com

www.theguardian.com

www.weforum.org

Glossary

Absolute poverty
Inability to meet even the most basic survival needs. This includes the necessities such as food, water, shelter, clothing and health care.

Austerity
In economic policy, austerity refers to a collection of political and economic measures aimed at reducing government budget deficits. These measures typically involve cuts in government spending, increases in taxes, or a combination of both.

Benefits
We use the term 'state benefits' to describe any money that is given to us by the Government. Benefits are paid to any member of the public who may need extra money to help them meet the costs of everyday living.

Budget
A financial plan used by governments, businesses or individuals to manage income and expenses.

Budget (Finance Bill)
The Budget is the statement delivered to the House of Commons each year by the Chancellor of the Exchequer which sets out the state of the nation's finances and any planned changes to taxation and spending.

Consumer
A consumer is anyone who purchases and uses goods and services.

Credit
A consumer can obtain goods and services before payment, based on an agreement that payment will be made at some point in the future. Other conditions may also be imposed. Forms of credit can include personal loans, overdrafts, credit cards, store cards, interest-free credit and hire purchase. However, reliance on credit can result in high levels of consumer debt.

Dietary inequality
Where inequalities in the food system mean people in low-income groups eat less healthily than those on higher incomes.

Economy
The way in which a region manages its resources. References to the 'national economy' indicate the financial situation of a country: how wealthy or prosperous it is.

Food bank
A place where food is given to people who do not have enough money to buy it, for example by a charity.

Household income
The combined amount of money earned by all members of a household.

Inflation
A measure of the rate of rising prices of goods and services in an economy.

Interest
A fee charged on borrowed money. It is usually calculated as a percentage of the sum borrowed and paid in regular instalments. An 'interest rate' refers to the amount of money charged on a borrowed amount over a given period. Interest can also be earned on money which is deposited in a bank account and is paid regularly by the bank to the account holder.

Living Wage
The Living Wage is a wage that is based on the cost-of-living and is set by the Living Wage Foundation. There is a UK rate and a London rate.

Loan
An amount of money that is borrowed and is expected to be paid back, usually with interest.

Poverty
Peter Townsend offers this definition of poverty: 'Individuals, families and groups in the population can be said to be in poverty when they lack the resources to obtain the types of diet, participate in the activities, and have the living conditions and amenities which are customary, or are at least widely encouraged and approved, in the societies in which they belong.'

Poverty line
The poverty line is the income level below which an individual can be said to be living in poverty. In the UK, the poverty line is defined as 60% of median household income, adjusted for household composition. Globally speaking, people are defined as living in absolute poverty if they have less than $1 (USD) a day to live on.

Recession
A period during which economic activity has slowed, causing a reduction in Gross Domestic Product (GDP), employment, household incomes and business profits. If GDP shows a reduction over at least six months, a country is then said to be in recession. Recessions are caused by people spending less, businesses making less and banks being more reluctant to give people loans.

Relative poverty
A measure of income inequality: dependent on social context, the standard of resources which is seen as socially acceptable in comparison with others in society. This differs between countries and over time. An income-related example would be living on less than 60% of the average UK income.

Tax
An amount of money paid to the Government that is based on your income or the cost of goods or services you have bought.

Universal Credit
Universal Credit is a payment to help with living costs. It was introduced in the Welfare Reform Act in 2012 as a means of combining six benefits including housing benefit, working tax credits and jobseeker's allowance, within one scheme.

Index

A
absolute poverty 1, 4–5, 14–15 *see also* destitution
abuse 3
Afghanistan 18–19

B
benefits
 adequate 3, 8, 9, 10, 16, 17
 means-tested 13
 two-child limit 14, 15, 17
 winter fuel payments 12

C
carers 8, 10
causes
 cost-of-living crisis 11
 poverty 1, 2–3
child poverty 4, 6, 9, 14–15, 29, 30–31
cycle of poverty 2

D
debt 1, 9, 26, 27
destitution 7, 14
digital poverty 29
disabled people 8
discrimination 3

E
education 1, 2
employment
 jobs 2–3, 8, 9–10, 24, 25
 unemployment 2, 8, 27
ethnicity 5, 8
Europe 20–23

F
family structure 3, 7, 14, 15, 17
food banks 16, 33, 34
food poverty 5, 14, 29, 32
food prices 20–21
fuel 12, 20–22, 27–28
fuel poverty 29

G
Gen Z 24–25
global impacts 12, 18–23, 24
greedflation 22–23

H
health 1, 17, 35, 36, 37
housing 1, 5, 8, 10, 16, 28
hygiene poverty 29, 35, 36–37

I
impacts
 cost-of-living crisis 12, 16–17
 poverty 1, 3
inequality, income 12, 28, 30–31
inflation 20–23, 24, 26–28

L
language of poverty 30–31
Lebanon 19
life expectancy 17

M
measuring poverty 4–5
mental health 35, 36, 37
millennials 24–25

P
pensioners 6, 10, 12, 14
period poverty 29, 36, 38, 39–40
poverty gap 8 *see also* inequality, income

R
regional variations 8–9, 10, 15
relative poverty 1, 4–5
respect for those in poverty 30–31

S
schools 34, 35
second jobs 24, 25
solutions
 cost-of-living crisis 13, 17, 27–28
 poverty 9–10, 30–31
Somalia 19
Sudan 18

T
trends over time 4–7
two-child benefit limit 14, 15, 17

U
unemployment 2, 8, 27

W
wages 2–3, 26, 27
winter fuel payments 12

Y
young adults 24–25